WILD AGE

STEVE PARKER

QEB Publishing

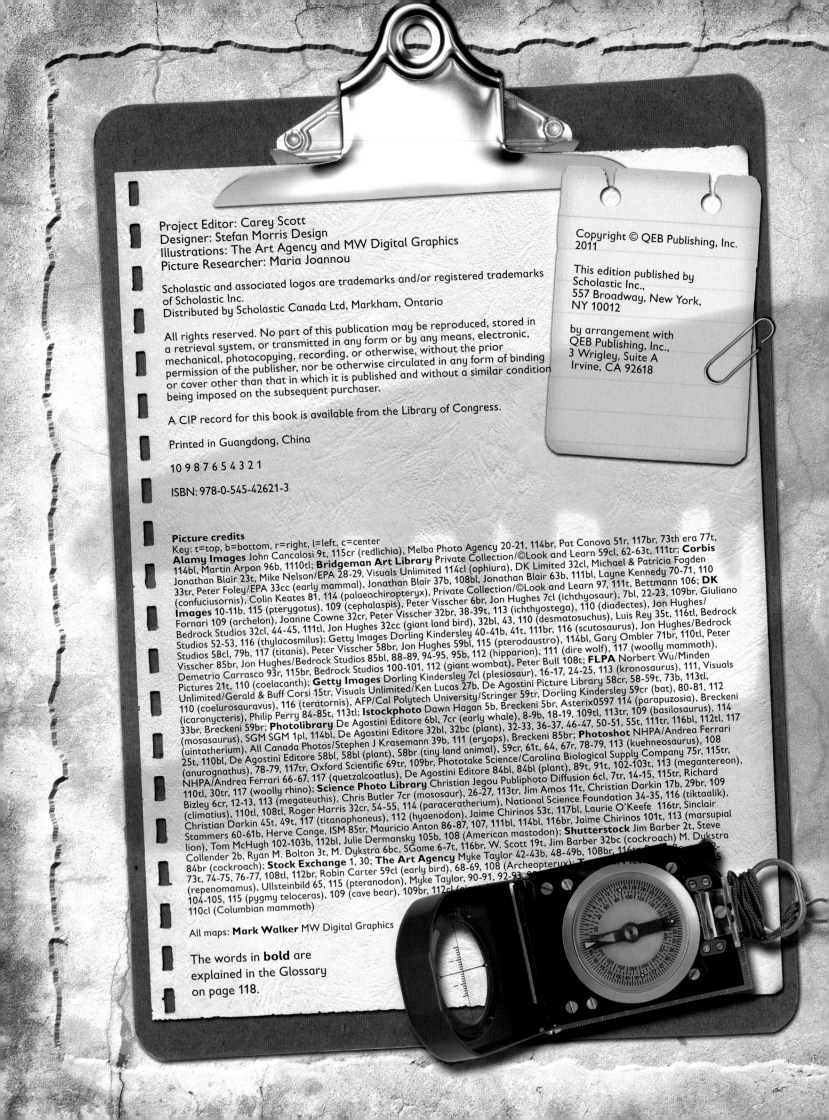

Project Editor: Carey Scott
Designer: Stefan Morris Design
Illustrations: The Art Agency and MW Digital Graphics
Picture Researcher: Maria Joannou

Printed in Guangdong, China

10 9 8 7 6 5 4 3 2 1

ISBN: 978-0-545-42621-3

Copyright © QEB Publishing, Inc.
2011

This edition published by
Scholastic Inc.,
557 Broadway, New York,
NY 10012

by arrangement with
QEB Publishing, Inc.,
3 Wrigley, Suite A
Irvine, CA 92618

Picture credits
Key: t=top, b=bottom, r=right, l=left, c=center
Alamy Images John Cancalosi 9t, 115cr (redlichia), Melba Photo Agency 20-21, 114br, Pat Canova 51r, 117br, 73th era 77t, 114bl, Martin Arpon 96b, 1110tl; **Bridgeman Art Library** Private Collection/©Look and Learn 59cl, 62-63t, 111tr; **Corbis** Jonathan Blair 23t, Mike Nelson/EPA 28-29, Visuals Unlimited 114cl (ophiura), DK Limited 32cl, Michael & Patricia Fogden 33tr, Peter Foley/EPA 33cc (early mammal), Jonathan Blair 37b, 108bl, Jonathan Blair 63b, 111bl, Layne Kennedy 70-71, 110 (confuciusornis), Colin Keates 81, 114 (palaeochiropteryx), Private Collection/©Look and Learn 97, 111t, Bettmann 106; **DK Images** 10-11b, 115 (pterygotus), 109 (cephalaspis), Peter Visscher 6br, Jon Hughes 7cl (ichthyosaur), 7bl, 22-23, 109br, Giuliano Fornari 109 (archelon), Joanne Cowne 32cr, Peter Visscher 32br, 38-39t, 113 (ichthyostega), 110 (diadectes), Jon Hughes/ Bedrock Studios 32cl, 44-45, 111tl, Jon Hughes 32cc (giant land bird), 32bl, 43, 110 (desmatosuchus), Luis Rey 35t, 116tl, Bedrock Studios 52-53, 116 (thylacosmilus); Getty Images Dorling Kindersley 40-41b, 41t, 111br, 116 (scutosaurus), Jon Hughes/Bedrock Studios 58cl, 79b, 117 (titanis), Peter Visscher 58br, Jon Hughes 59bl, 115 (pterodaustro), 114bl, Gary Ombler 71br, 110tl, Peter Visscher 85br, Jon Hughes/Bedrock Studios 85bl, 88-89, 94-95, 95b, 112 (hipparion), 111 (dire wolf), 117 (woolly mammoth), Demetrio Carrasco 93r, 115br, Bedrock Studios 100-101, 112 (giant wombat), Peter Bull 108t; **FLPA** Norbert Wu/Minden Pictures 21t, 110 (coelacanth); **Getty Images** Dorling Kindersley 7cl (plesiosaur), 16-17, 24-25, 113 (kronosaurus), 111, Visuals Unlimited/Gerald & Buff Corsi 15tr, Visuals Unlimited/Ken Lucas 27b, De Agostini Picture Library 58cr, 58-59t, 73b, 113tl, 110 (coelurosauravus), 116 (teratornis), AFP/Cal Polytech University/Stringer 59tr, Dorling Kindersley 59cr (bat), 80-81, 112 (icaronycteris), Philip Perry 84-85t, 113tl; **Istockphoto** Dawn Hagan 5b, Breckeni 5br, Asterix0597 114 (parapuzosia), Breckeni 33br, Breckeni 59br; **Photolibrary** De Agostini Editore 6bl, 7cr (early whale), 8-9b, 18-19, 109tl, 113tr, 109 (basilosaurus), 114 (mosasaurus), SGM SGM 1pl, 114bl, De Agostini Editore 32bl, 32bc (plant), 32-33, 36-37, 46-47, 50-51, 55t, 111tr, 116bl, 112tl, 117 (uintatherium), All Canada Photos/Stephen J Krasemann 39b, 111 (eryops), Breckeni 85br; **Photoshot** NHPA/Andrea Ferrari 25t, 110bl, De Agostini Editore 58bl, 58bl (plant), 58br (tiny land animal), 59cr, 61t, 64, 67r, 78-79, 113 (kuehneosaurus), 108 (anurognathus), 78-79, 117tr, Oxford Scientific 69tr, 109br, Phototake Science/Carolina Biological Supply Company 75r, 115tr, NHPA/Andrea Ferrari 66-67, 117 (quetzalcoatlus), De Agostini Editore 84bl, 84bl (plant), 89t, 91t, 102-103t, 113 (megantereon), 110tl, 30tr, 117 (woolly rhino); **Science Photo Library** Christian Jegou Publiphoto Diffusion 6cl, 7tr, 14-15, 115tr, Richard Bizley 6cr, 12-13, 113 (megateuthis), Chris Butler 7cr (mososaur), 26-27, 113tr, Jim Amos 11t, Christian Darkin 17b, 29br, 109 (climatius), 110tl, 108tl, Roger Harris 32cr, 54-55, 114 (paraceratherium), National Science Foundation 34-35, 116 (tiktaalik), Christian Darkin 45t, 49t, 117 (titanophoneus), 112 (hyaenodon), Jaime Chirinos 53r, 117bl, Laurie O'Keefe 116tr, Sinclair Stammers 60-61b, Herve Conge, ISM 85tr, Mauricio Anton 86-87, 107, 111bl, 114bl, 116br, Jaime Chirinos 101t, 113 (marsupial lion), Tom McHugh 102-103b, 112bl, Julie Dermansky 105b, 108 (American mastodon); **Shutterstock** Jim Barber 2t, Steve Collender 2b, Ryan M. Bolton 3t, M. Dykstra 6bc, SGame 6-7t, 116br, W. Scott 19t, Jim Barber 32bc (cockroach) M. Dykstra 84br (cockroach); **Stock Exchange** 1, 30; **The Art Agency** Myke Taylor 42-43b, 48-49b, 108br, 116tr, 73t, 74-75, 76-77, 108tl, 112br, Robin Carter 59cl (early bird), 68-69, 108 (Archeopteryx); **T** (repenomamus), Ullsteinbild 65, 115 (pteranodon), Myke Taylor, 90-91, 92-93, 104-105, 115 (pygmy teloceras), 109 (cave bear), 109br, 112cl (si 110cl (Columbian mammoth)

All maps: **Mark Walker** MW Digital Graphics

The words in **bold** are
explained in the Glossary
on page 118.

CONTENTS

DIVE UNDER THE WAVES
WITH ICHTHYOSAURS...
MEET GIANT
SEA-SCORPIONS...
SWIM WITH THE
FIRST FISHES...

JELLY MONSTERS

The first living things began in the oceans more than 3 billion years ago. They were too tiny to see. Over millions of years they became larger and more complicated—the sea's first mini-monsters.

These early animals had no teeth, legs, or shells. They had soft bodies and looked like today's jellyfish and worms. The biggest were the size of your thumb, such as *Spriggina*.

Such strange creatures probably wriggled along the seabed or drifted in the water. What did they eat? No one really knows. Perhaps mud, or the first seaweeds—or maybe each other!

◗ *Spriggina* had a curved head, lots of body sections, called segments, and a narrow tail.

◖ **Prehistoric time** is divided into periods, which have their own names. Each period started and ended a certain number of millions of years ago (mya).

First ammonites
410 mya

510 mya
The first fish appear

Ediacaran	Cambrian	Ordovician	Silurian	Devonian	Carboniferous	Permian
before 542 mya	542–488 mya	488–444 mya	444–416 mya	416–359 mya	359–299 mya	299–251 mya

550 mya   500 mya   400 mya   300 mya

540 mya Shelled sea animals   **460 mya** Land plants   **430 mya** Tiny land animals   **360 mya** Four-legged land animals

◗ Strange living things that looked like leaves, feathers, cushions, and plates grew on the seabed 550 million years ago. There were no fish, sea snails, or crabs.

Ichthyosaurs appear

Early plesiosaurs

First mosasaurs

Early whales

240 mya   **200 mya**   **100 mya**   **50 mya**

Triassic 251–200 mya	**Jurassic** 200–145 mya	**Cretaceous** 145–65 mya	**Palaeogene** 65–23 mya	**Neogene** 23–2.6 mya	**Quaternary** 2.6 mya–now

200 mya   100 mya   NOW

230 mya Early dinosaurs

65 mya Mass extinction kills off most land and many sea animals.

SHIELD SHELLS

About 530 million years ago, many new animals appeared in the seas. Most were small but fierce, and they had a new feature—a shell!

Shells protected their wearers against enemies. Once the animals died, their shells formed **fossils**—remains of once-living things, preserved in the rocks and turned to stone.

The largest hunter of the time, *Anomalocaris*, was probably bigger than you! It swam by waving its fan-shaped tail and side flaps, and it grabbed **prey** with its two long spiked "arms." Its round mouth had many teeth to pull in and chew up its meal.

WILD FILE

Anomalocaris

GROUP Anomalocaridid

WHEN Cambrian Period

FOOD Hard-shelled creatures

FOSSIL SITES North America including Canada, China, Australia

● Fossil sites

⬤ Watching with its two big eyes, *Anomalocaris* pushes a smaller creature into its round mouth using its two feeding arms.

HOW BIG?

Anomalocaris
Up to 3.3 feet (1 meter) long

◑ **Trilobites** such as *Redlichia* were among the first animals to have eyes and strong shells—especially over the head end.

WILD!

Until 1985, scientists thought that fossils of separate parts of *Anomalocaris* were from three different animals—a jellyfish, a sponge, and a shrimp.

SCORPIONS OF THE SEA

About 420 million years ago, giant scorpions became the seas' rulers. They were some of the most powerful predators of their time.

Sea scorpions did not have a poison tail sting like today's land scorpions. But they did have big eyes to see their prey and two very strong pincers to grab a victim and tear it apart.

Sea scorpions could crawl about on their eight legs and were able to breathe air like some of today's crabs. They could also swim by swishing their paddle-like rear legs to move and their fan-shaped tail to steer.

HOW BIG?

Pterygotus
7.2 feet (2.2 meters) long

WILD FILE

Pterygotus

GROUP Sea scorpions (Eurypterids)

WHEN Late Silurian

FOOD Fish

WHERE Worldwide, especially North America and Europe

Fossil sites

◖ Brittle stars are types of bendy-armed starfish. As long as 450 million years ago they covered the seabed in huge numbers, eating tiny bits of food in the mud.

CLOSE COUSINS

Sea scorpions were members of the **arachnid** group—cousins of today's scorpions and spiders as well as mites, ticks, and horseshoe and king crabs.

● The huge nippers of **Pterygotus** could stab and tear apart almost any creature of the time—including its own young.

CURLS AND CONES

The first curly-shelled ammonites hunted in the seas about 400 million years ago. They swam fast by squirting out a jet of water, just like today's squid.

An **ammonite**'s shell shape is called a spiral. As the ammonite grew, it made a new, wider section at the shell's open end. This became the ammonite's home. It had big eyes and more than 20 tentacles to grab its prey.

Belemnites were similar to ammonites, but most had ten tentacles and a body shaped like an ice cream cone. Some belemnites were as long as a family car!

◗ These are fossils of shells from **Orthoceras**, a creature called a **nautiloid**. It looked like a long, straight ammonite.

WILD FILE

Parapuzosia

GROUP Ammonites—Cephalopods

WHEN Late Cretaceous Period

FOOD Fish, crabs

WHERE Europe, North America

● Fossil sites

HOW BIG?

Parapuzosia
8.2 feet (2.5 meters)
across

● *Parapuzosia*'s main body was inside the end of its coiled shell. If the ammonite was in danger, it could hide its tentacles in the shell, too, in the same way that snails pull themselves into their shells.

FIRST FISH

Today, there are millions of fish in the sea. But, until about 510 million years ago, there were no fish at all.

The first fish had no jaws in their mouths so they could not bite and chew. The mouth was probably a thin slit or rounded opening, through which the fish sucked in its food.

These **jawless fish** did not have movable fins like later fish, but their streamlined bodies enabled them to swim well. They were protected from predators by a hard head shield and bony scales along the back. Some could live in the sea and swim into rivers, too.

WILD FILE

Pteraspis

GROUP	Jawless fish—Agnathans
WHEN	Early Devonian Period
FOOD	Worms, other small creatures
WHERE	Europe

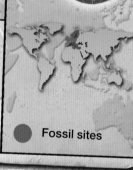

● Fossil sites

HOW BIG?

Pteraspis
7.9 inches (20 centimeters) long

WILD!

Fossils of jawless fish from 480 million years ago were found in the desert in the middle of Australia, which is now more than 930 miles (1,500 kilometers) from the sea!

◐ Two kinds of jawless fish still exist today—lampreys and hagfish. They suck blood and scrape flesh from other animals. The hagfish is soft and pink and it can cover itself with its own thick slime in a few seconds.

◑ The early fish **Pteraspis**, with its nose and back horns, swims along at the top of this ancient sea scene. Lower left is one of its jawless cousins, **Arandaspis.**

MONSTERS IN THE DEEP

As more fish appeared in the seas, some kinds grew larger. One of the biggest was Dunkleosteus, which was as long as a bus.

Dunkleosteus had thick armor plates of bone over its head and neck for protection. The rest of its body was probably not well protected. But a fish this huge had few enemies!

The teeth of *Dunkleosteus* were fearsome sharp blades of bone. They could easily slice through the armor of other **hard-bodied animals**.

HOW BIG?

Dunkleosteus
32.8 feet (10 meters)

◗ *Dunkleosteus* weighed more than 3 tons, which is four times heavier than today's great white shark. Its bite was as powerful as that of the dinosaur *Tyrannosaurus rex.*

WILD FILE

Dunkleosteus

GROUP Armored fish—Placoderms

WHEN Late Devonian Period

FOOD Sharks, other fish, ammonites

FOSSIL SITES North Africa, Europe, North America

● Fossil sites

◗ *Bothriolepsis* had bony body armor, like *Dunkleosteus.* This fish was only 11.8 inches (30 centimeters) long. It probably lived in rivers, not in the sea.

SHARK GIANTS

True sharks appeared more than 400 million years ago, and all were fierce hunters. Spiny sharks were another group of early fish.

Spiny sharks were not really sharks, but they did have sharklike, streamlined bodies and sharp spines. They had thorns in their fins and skin to protect them from predators. They probably ate fish, shellfish, and worms.

The biggest of the **true sharks** was *Megalodon*, which hunted in the seas until about 1.5 million years ago. It was similar to today's great white—but three times longer and 20 times heavier!

WILD FILE

Megalodon

GROUP Sharks —Selachians
WHEN Neogene Period
FOOD Large sea animals
WHERE Worldwide

● Fossil sites

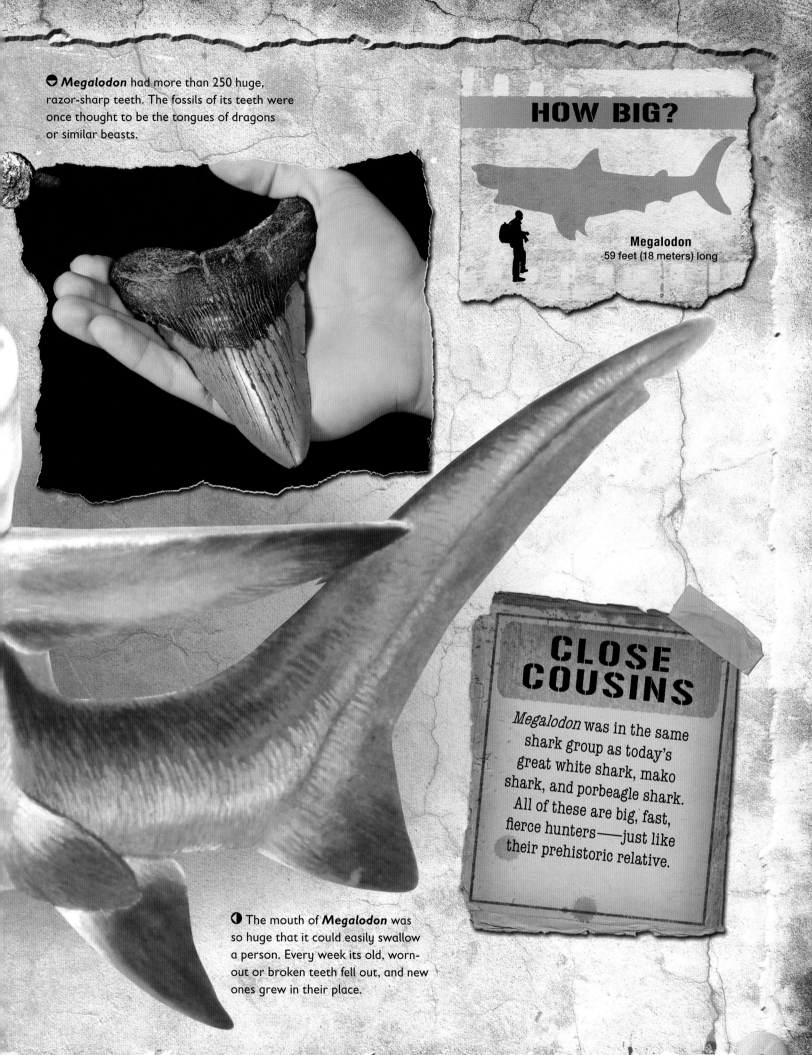

● *Megalodon* had more than 250 huge, razor-sharp teeth. The fossils of its teeth were once thought to be the tongues of dragons or similar beasts.

Megalodon
59 feet (18 meters) long

CLOSE COUSINS

Megalodon was in the same shark group as today's great white shark, mako shark, and porbeagle shark. All of these are big, fast, fierce hunters——just like their prehistoric relative.

◑ The mouth of *Megalodon* was so huge that it could easily swallow a person. Every week its old, worn-out or broken teeth fell out, and new ones grew in their place.

FISHY FINS

Gradually, over millions of years, fish developed in different ways to become better, faster swimmers and more efficient hunters.

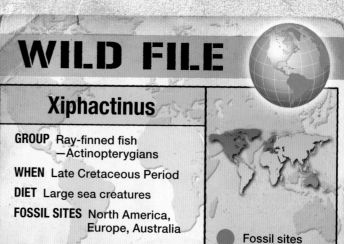
Some fish grew fins that spread out like fans, for better swimming control. One of the biggest of these was *Xiphactinus*. This fierce **predator** had pointed fangs up to 3.9 inches (10 centimeters) long.

Other fish, called **lobe-fin fish**, had fins with fleshy, muscular bases. They could use these to crawl across land from one pool to another. Gradually some of them became the first four-legged land animals.

HOW BIG?

Xiphactinus
16.4 feet (5 meters) long

◐ Lobe-fin fish, called coelacanths, lived more than 70 million years ago. Two kinds are still around today, swimming in the deep waters of the Indian Ocean.

⬤ **Xiphactinus** was a long, slim, speedy hunter. It died out with the dinosaurs, 65 million years ago.

WILD!

Inside one fossil of *Xiphactinus* was the fossil of another fish it had just eaten. This fish, *Gillicus*, was 5.9 feet (1.8 meters) long— bigger than you!

SPEEDY KILLERS

While dinosaurs ruled the land, from 230 million years ago, new monsters took over the seas. Fastest were the "fish lizards," the ichthyosaurs.

On the outside, **ichthyosaurs** looked like dolphins. But they were in the same group as dinosaurs—the reptiles. They came to the surface to breathe through the mouth or the nostrils (nose holes) in front of the eyes.

Ichthyosaurs swished their tails from side to side to swim at speeds of up to 25 mph (40 kph). They grabbed their prey in their long, slim jaws.

WILD FILE

Shonisaurus

GROUP Ichthyosaurs
WHEN Late Triassic Period
DIET Fish, squid
FOSSIL SITES North America, Asia

Fossil sites

HOW BIG?

Shonisaurus
65 feet (20 meters) long

CLOSE COUSINS

Ichthyosaurs might look like dolphins, or fish, or even crocodiles. But these are not close relatives. Their nearest cousins are lizards and snakes in the reptile group.

⬤ The first complete ichthyosaur fossil to be discovered was named Ichthyosaurus. It was quite small, just 6.5 feet (2 meters) long.

◔ The giant ichthyosaur *Shonisaurus* was one of the largest hunters that ever lived in the sea. It had a back fin like a dolphin and four flipper-like limbs for steering— dolphins have only two.

NECKS AND FLIPPERS

During the Age of the Dinosaurs, enormous reptiles called plesiosaurs hunted in the oceans. Some had teeth as long as carving knives!

There were two main kinds of **plesiosaurs**, and both swam by flapping their huge flippers. The long-necked types could easily grab fish and other animals to eat up.

Short-necked plesiosaurs, called **pliosaurs**, had a short neck but a massive head and jaws. They were **top predators** and could eat almost any victims, including big fish, sea turtles, ichthyosaurs, and other plesiosaurs.

WILD FILE

Kronosaurus

GROUP Pliosaurs—short-necked
Plesiosaurs

WHEN Early Cretaceous Period

DIET Large sea creatures

FOSSIL SITES Australia,
South America

● Fossil sites

Elasmosaurus was 45 feet (14 meters) long, and more than half the length was its neck. It darted out its head like a snake to snap at creatures such as ammonites.

Kronosaurus probably swam mainly with its front flippers, using the back ones for bursts of speed. Each tooth was bigger than your hand, but fairly blunt, for crushing rather than cutting.

WILD!

Newly discovered fossils known as Predator X may be from the most massive pliosaur ever discovered. This giant could have been 50 feet (15 meters) long and 55 tons in weight.

MOUTHFUL OF TEETH

As plesiosaurs and ichthyosaurs died out, near the end of the Age of the Dinosaurs, a new kind of monster came to rule the seas—the mosasaur.

Mosasaurs were some of the biggest, fastest, strongest ocean hunters ever. Their long jaws were full of sharp cone-shaped teeth, which they used to tear their prey apart.

Like pliosaurs and ichthyosaurs, mosasaurs stayed near the surface to breathe air. They could not walk on land with their flippers, so they stayed in the sea, and even gave birth to their babies there.

HOW BIG?

Mosasaurus
50 feet (15 meters) long

CLOSE COUSINS

Mosasaurs looked similar to crocodiles. But their nearest relatives today are the types of lizards called monitors. This group includes the world's biggest lizard, the Komodo dragon.

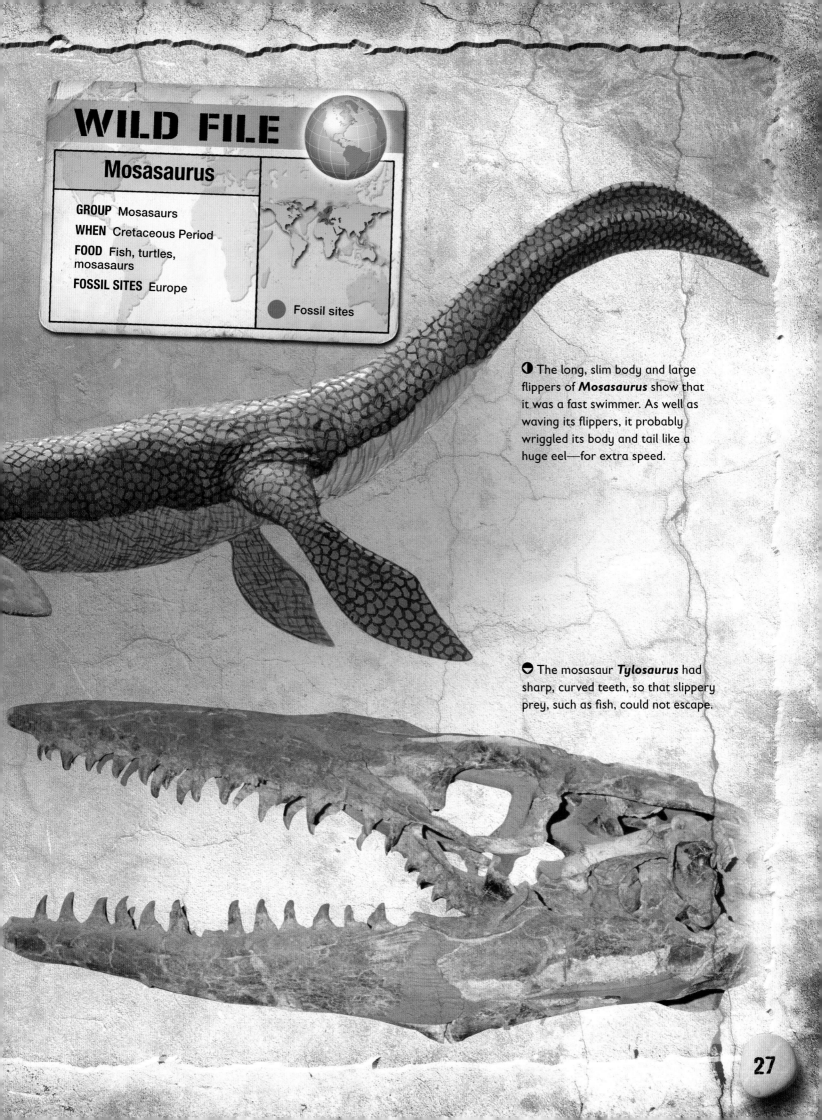

WILD FILE

Mosasaurus

GROUP Mosasaurs

WHEN Cretaceous Period

FOOD Fish, turtles, mosasaurs

FOSSIL SITES Europe

● Fossil sites

◗ The long, slim body and large flippers of *Mosasaurus* show that it was a fast swimmer. As well as waving its flippers, it probably wriggled its body and tail like a huge eel—for extra speed.

◒ The mosasaur *Tylosaurus* had sharp, curved teeth, so that slippery prey, such as fish, could not escape.

BACK TO THE SEA

Many reptile sea monsters died out along with the dinosaurs, 65 million years ago. Soon, their place was taken by mammals that had left the land and gone into the water.

At first, all mammals lived on land. By about 55 million years ago, some were splashing along the seashore and hunting in the shallows. These were the first whales and dolphins.

Gradually, the whales' front legs became flippers. They lost their back legs and grew wide tail flukes for swimming. The whales alive now are the biggest sea creatures of all time.

◗ These fossil experts are digging up the remains of *Basilosaurus*, including its long backbone, from the desert sands of North Africa.

HOW BIG?

Basilosaurus
Up to 82 feet (25 meters) long

WILD FILE

Basilosaurus

GROUP Whales—cetaceans
WHEN Middle Paleogene Period
FOOD Fish to large sea creatures
WHERE North America, Africa, Asia

● Fossil sites

Ambulocetus was almost a whale and a good swimmer. But it still had four legs so that it could walk on land. Its fossils came from Pakistan in Asia.

DISCOVER THE FIRST ANIMALS
TO LIVE ON THE LAND...

WALK WITH
PREHISTORIC GIANTS...

MEET SABER-TOOTHED
HUNTERS...

FIRST ONTO LAND

Long, long ago, the first strange jelly-like creatures swam in the sea. Then came shelled animals and early fish. But the land was bare, with no life at all.

From about 460 million years ago, plants began to grow from the water's edge up onto the land. They spread and thrived. When the plants died, they rotted into the sand and mud, making the soil rich for bigger plants to grow.

Next, the first animals crawled from the water onto the land to eat the plants. They were tiny bugs such as insects and **mites**, smaller than this "o."

Gradually, land plants grew into the first trees. Land creatures became larger, too. The giant millipede *Arthropleura* was as big as your bed!

First trees

385 mya

First reptiles

310 mya

Ediacaran before 542 mya	Cambrian 542–488 mya	Ordovician 488–444 mya	Silurian 444–416 mya	Devonian 416–359 mya	Carboniferous 359–299 mya	Permian 299–251 mya

550 mya   500 mya   400 mya   300 mya

540 mya   460 mya   430 mya   360 mya

Shelled sea animals   Land plants   Tiny land animals   Shelled sea animals

A creature now living which looks like some of the early land animals is the velvet worm. It lives in damp forests and is squishy and wriggly, but it also has lots of stumpy, bendy legs for walking.

Arthropleura had a hard body-covering and more than 40 legs. It probably ate bits of plants and small creatures, such as worms and bugs.

Mammal-like reptiles appear

Early mammals

Giant land birds

Biggest-ever land animals

45 mya   30 mya

50 mya

200 mya

Triassic 251–200 mya	Jurassic 200–145 mya	Cretaceous 145–65 mya	Palaeogene 65–23 mya	Neogene 23–2.6 mya	Quaternary 2.6 mya–now

200 mya   100 mya   NOW

230 mya

65 mya

Early dinosaurs

Mass extinction kills off most land and many sea animals.

FINS TO LEGS

From about 380 million years ago, new kinds of creatures appeared. They began to poke their heads out of the water and wriggle toward the shore.

These animals were still fish. But they could breathe air using lungs, as well as breathe in water. They could also pull themselves along on land using their fins, which had strong muscles—almost like legs.

Tiktaalik was one of these strange four-legged fish. It probably lived in swamps, snapping up **prey,** such as worms and smaller fish, with its sharp teeth.

WILD!

Most fish have a head that merges straight into the body, without a neck. But *Tiktaalik* could bend its head on its body, making it the first fish with a neck!

HOW BIG?

Tiktaalik
8.2 feet (2.5 meters) long

◑ The fishy creature *Panderichthys* was 47 inches (120 centimeters) long. Its two front leglike fins were bigger and stronger than the two back ones.

◒ The fins of *Tiktaalik* had small, slim bones inside that were similar to the finger and toe bones of later creatures.

WILD FILE

Tiktaalik

GROUP Fish—lobe-fin fish
WHEN Devonian Period
FOOD Smaller water creatures
FOSSIL SITES North America, including Canada

● Fossil sites

FIRST ON FOUR LEGS

Many land animals, from lizards to elephants, run around on four legs. But the first creatures with four legs didn't run at all.

Animals called **tetrapods** have a backbone inside the body and four legs. (Some have two arms and two legs, like…you!) The legs and toes of tetrapods were first used in water, perhaps for crawling through thick weeds. Only later did they become useful for moving on land.

Early tetrapods were *Ichthyostega* and *Acanthostega*. They could breathe air and waddle about on dry ground. The land was getting busier!

WILD FILE

Ichthyostega

GROUP Tetrapods

WHEN Late Devonian Period

FOOD Small animals

FOSSIL SITES Greenland

Fossil sites

HOW BIG?

Ichthyostega
5 feet (1.5 meters) long

◑ Ichthyostega was halfway between a water creature and a land animal. It probably sunbathed to warm up, then dived into the water to hunt prey, like a giant slimy newt.

◑ This fossil skull (head bone) of Acanthostega shows its many small, sharp teeth. They were used to catch animal food such as fish and water bugs.

LAND INVASION

As four-legged animals spread over the land, they changed or evolved into many different kinds. One of the biggest and toughest was *Diadectes*.

We know how animals changed in the past from their fossils. These are remains of once-living things preserved in the rocks and turned to stone. Fossils show that *Diadectes* was large and heavy, with strong legs for running.

HOW BIG?

Diadectes
9.8 feet (3 meters) long

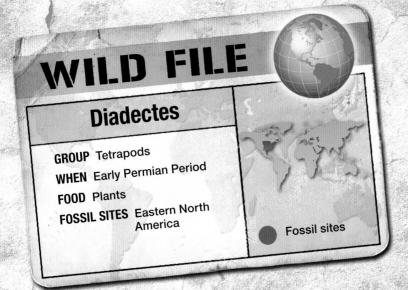

WILD FILE

Diadectes

GROUP Tetrapods
WHEN Early Permian Period
FOOD Plants
FOSSIL SITES Eastern North America

Fossil sites

Diadectes had lots of teeth, but these were not sharp. The front teeth were like a rake for gathering leaves, which the wide back teeth chewed before swallowing.

● *Diadectes* was one of the first really big plant-eaters on land. It was also one of the first to hold its body off the ground on its strong legs.

◐ *Eryops* the tetrapod was 6.5 feet (2 meters) long. It had a very thick skull bone and strong legs for running. It could open its big mouth wide to grab many kinds of prey.

CLOSE COUSINS

Diadectes was a cousin of the living animals called **amphibians**. It was about three times heavier than today's largest amphibian, the Chinese giant salamander.

SUNNY SAILS

As more animals crowded onto the land, staying alive became difficult—especially when fearsome *Dimetrodon* was around!

Dimetrodon was one of the biggest animals of its time. Its long, sharp teeth were the sign of a fierce hunter. On its back was a tall flap of skin, like a ship's sail, held up by thin rods of bone.

Dimetrodon was probably **cold-blooded**, like all animals of its time. In the early morning, its sail would soak up the sun's heat. So, *Dimetrodon* would warm up quickly and be able to chase after colder, slower prey.

HOW BIG?

Dimetrodon
11.5 feet (3.5 meters) long

The plant-eater *Scutosaurus* was as big as a horse, but much heavier. It was protected from attack by hard scalelike plates, called **scutes,** in its skin.

The legs of *Dimetrodon* were at the sides of its body, rather than underneath, as in a dinosaur. So, while the dinosaurs could walk in an upright way, *Dimetrodon* walked with a waddle, like a lizard.

WILD FILE

Dimetrodon

GROUP Tetrapods
WHEN Permian Period
FOOD Big animals
FOSSIL SITES North America, Europe

Fossil sites

OPEN WIDE!

In 2001, fossils of the biggest-ever crocodile were found in the Sahara. What was it doing in the world's largest desert?

About 110 million years ago, in the **Age of the Dinosaurs**, the Sahara was very different. It was a region of tropical forests and woods with lots of rivers, lakes, and streams. Here lived *Sarcosuchus*—a giant crocodile as long as a bus, with a mouth the size of a doorway.

Sarcosuchus probably hunted in the water for fish. It might also have come onto land to attack and eat baby dinosaurs.

WILD!

The biggest crocodile today is the saltwater croc. *Sarcosuchus* was twice as long and five times heavier. If *Sarcosuchus* were alive today, it could eat a "saltie" for breakfast!

◐ *Sarcosuchus* might have waited in the water for young dinosaurs and other animals to come and drink. Then, it would leap out and attack them.

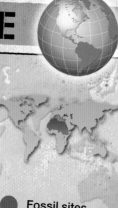

WILD FILE

Sarcosuchus

GROUP Reptiles—crocodiles
WHEN Cretaceous Period
FOOD Medium-sized animals
FOSSIL SITES North Africa

 Fossil sites

Sarcosuchus
Around 39 feet (12 meters) long

● *Desmatosuchus* looked like a flesh-eating crocodile. But it was a different kind of creature called an **aetosaur,** and it fed on plants.

HUGE HORNS

As land creatures became more varied, some developed strange features. One of the weirdest-looking of them all was *Estemmenosuchus*.

Estemmenosuchus was the size of today's rhinoceros, with massive, powerful muscles in its legs and chest. It had a big mouth and sharp teeth. Its huge head horns were not long and sharp, but made of flat parts sticking out at odd angles.

WILD FILE

Estemmenosuchus

GROUP Tetrapods—therapsids, or mammal-like reptiles

WHEN Permian Period

FOOD Not known. Plants, animals or perhaps both

FOSSIL SITES Russia

Fossil sites

● Fossils of the skin of *Estemmenosuchus* have no reptilelike scales, so it may have had hair, like a mammal. It belonged to an in-between group of animals called **mammal-like reptiles**.

Almost 10 feet (3 meters) long, *Titanophoneus* was a slim, speedy meat-eater. Like *Estemmenosuchus*, it belonged to the mammal-like reptile group of animals.

WILD!

A herd of *Estemmenosuchus* may have used their horns to fight each other at breeding time. Imagine the noise as their enormous heads banged and crashed together!

HOW BIG?

Estemmenosuchus
13 feet (4 meters) long

THE FIRST FURRY KILLERS

As well as mammal-like reptiles, there were also furry, warm-blooded creatures called mammals.

The first mammals probably developed from small mammal-like reptiles more than 200 million years ago. In the beginning, they were rat-sized, and they ate small creatures, such as worms and bugs.

Gradually, some mammals grew bigger, although none were larger than a big pet dog of today. Some of them could have eaten dinosaur eggs or even baby dinosaurs.

HOW BIG?

Cynognathus
3.3 feet (1 meter) long

WILD FILE

Cynognathus

GROUP Therapsids, or mammal-like reptiles

WHEN Early–Mid Triassic Period

FOOD Animal prey

FOSSIL SITES South America, South Africa, East Asia

Fossil sites

WILD!

One fossilized *Repenomamus* was preserved with the remains of a baby dinosaur, *Psittacosaurus*, inside its body. Was the little dinosaur the last meal of *Repenomamus*?

Fossils of *Repenomamus* discovered in China show that it was one of the largest mammals of its time—similar in size and shape to today's badger. It lived in the middle of the Age of the Dinosaurs, 130 million years ago.

Cynognathus had strong jaws and sharp teeth, like a wolf. It probably hunted small prey and chewed the already-dead bodies of big animals.

DEADLY HUNTERS

The Age of the Dinosaurs ended 65 million years ago. The land was quiet for a time. Soon, new kinds of animals appeared, such as the frightening bearlike *Sarkastodon*.

Sarkastodon looked like a combination of bear and dog. It had massively wide, strong teeth to chew meat and crush bones. It belonged to a group of predators called **creodonts**.

Other creodonts included the wolflike *Hyaenodon* and *Oxyaena*, which was similar to a large cat. Despite their size and power, all creodonts died out by about eight million years ago.

HOW BIG?

Sarkastodon
Length 9.8 feet (3 meters)

WILD FILE

Sarkastodon

GROUP Mammals—creodonts
WHEN Paleogene Period
FOOD Animals
FOSSIL SITES Central Asia

Fossil sites

◗ Unlike a bear, *Sarkastodon* had a long tail. But like a bear, it walked on the flat parts (or soles) of its feet. Probably it was a slow mover, not a fast runner.

❶ *Hyaenodon* had a long, thin snout with sharp teeth. Maybe it howled at night, like today's wolves and coyotes!

WILD!

Sarkastodon had plenty of big animals to hunt. Living at the same time and in the same region were rhinos and creatures called chalicotheres, which were cousins of today's horses.

TERROR BIRDS

After the dinosaurs, most of the big, strong animals on land were mammals. Yet, there were also great birds who could put up a good fight.

Gastornis was as tall as an ostrich, but much stronger and heavier. Its sharp beak had a hooked tip, like an eagle. Its legs were very powerful with pointed claws on the toes.

Gastornis was probably a fast-running predator. It chased after smaller animals, kicked and scratched them with its claws, then pecked them to death and tore them apart with its huge beak.

WILD FILE

Gastornis

GROUP Birds—flightless
WHEN Paleogene Period
FOOD Animal prey
FOSSIL SITES North America, Europe

● Fossil sites

HOW BIG?

Gastornis
Height 6.9 feet
(2.1 meters)

◗ The wings of *Gastornis* were much too small and weak for flight. This **flightless bird** may have had soft, hairlike feathers rather than the broad, stiff feathers of flying birds.

Titanis was a fierce hunting bird that could not fly—like *Gastornis*, but even bigger! Its fossils were found in North America and are about three million years old.

CLOSE COUSINS

Gastornis might have looked like a very strong, hook-beaked ostrich or an eagle with tiny wings. But its nearest relatives today are barnyard ducks and geese.

SABER TEETH!

For animals that kill to eat, the best weapons are teeth. *Thylacosmilus* certainly had big teeth!

Thylacosmilus looked like a big cat, with sharp claws, but it was in a different animal group, the **marsupials**. Its long upper teeth were curved like the type of sword called a saber. With its mouth closed, these upper teeth fit into flaps in the lower jaw for protection.

Thylacosmilus may have stabbed its victims to death with its saber teeth. Or it could have slashed at them to cause terrible flesh wounds, so they bled to death.

WILD FILE

Thylacosmilus

GROUP Mammals—marsupial-like

WHEN Neogene Period

FOOD Animal prey

FOSSIL SITES South America

● Fossil sites

◗ *Andrewsarchus* was a giant mammal predator more than 13 feet (4 meters) long and taller than a person. It lived about 40 million years ago.

CLOSE COUSINS

Thylacosmilus was related to marsupials, or pouched mammals, whose babies grow in the mother's pocket of skin. Its near cousins today are opossums, wombats, koalas, and kangaroos!

◖ *Thylacosmilus* would have leaped at its prey. With its huge claws ready to rip its victim's flesh and its massive saber teeth bared, it would have been a terrifying sight.

HOW BIG?

Thylacosmilus
5 feet (1.5 meters) long

BIGGEST EVER

Today's biggest land animal is the elephant. Millions of years ago, much bigger creatures roamed the world—including a giant hornless rhinoceros.

Paraceratherium was one of the largest-ever land animals, weighing up to 22 tons—four times heavier than an elephant. Like many other rhinos that lived long ago, it had no horn on its nose.

Paraceratherium's head was 25 feet (7.5 meters) above the ground—6.5 feet (2 meters) higher than a giraffe's. This vast beast was a gentle giant, munching leaves, twigs, and fruit from the treetops.

WILD!

Paraceratherium was so huge that it weighed more than some of the giant dinosaurs that lived 100 million years before it. But the dinosaurs were three times longer.

◑ Another plant-eater, *Uintatherium,* was about as big as the rhinoceros of today. It had a bumpy head and two tusks for fighting enemies. ***Uintatherium*** lived around 40 million years ago.

◒ *Paraceratherium* had a very long, bendy upper lip and probably a long tongue, too. So, it could reach even higher into the branches to pull off leaves.

WILD FILE

Paraceratherium

GROUP Mammals—rhinos

WHEN Late Paleogene and Neogene Periods

FOOD Tree leaves and other plants

FOSSIL SITES East Europe, Asia

● Fossil sites

HOW BIG?

Paraceratherium
Up to 29.5 feet (9 meters) long

DISCOVER THE
FIRST FLIERS...

MEET GIANT
PTEROSAURS...

SOAR WITH
PREHISTORIC BIRDS...

THE FIRST FLIERS

Today, there are thousands of different flying creatures—many kinds of birds, bats at nighttime, and flies, butterflies, and other insects. But long ago, the skies were empty.

The first fliers, more than 350 million years ago, were probably tiny bugs. They were similar to the dragonflies of today, but much smaller. We know about them from their fossils—body parts preserved in the rocks and turned to stone.

The biggest-ever flying bug was *Meganeura* from 300 million years ago. With wings 29.5 inches (75 centimeters) across, it was more than three times larger than today's dragonflies. It swooped down to catch smaller bugs on the ground and among plants.

◗ *Meganeura* was the size of today's big birds, such as crows. It had plenty of bugs, worms, and other food in the warm, wet swamps of the Carboniferous Period.

Early winged bugs

360 mya   300 mya

Giant dragonflie

Ediacaran	Cambrian	Ordovician	Silurian	Devonian	Carboniferous	Permi
before 542 mya	542–488 mya	488–444 mya	444–416 mya	416–359 mya	359–299 mya	299–251 m

550 mya   500 mya   400 mya   300 mya

540 mya Shelled sea animals   **460 mya** Land plants   **430 mya** Tiny land animals   **360 mya** Four-legged land animals

⬤ This bee is many millions of years old. But it is preserved in a substance called **amber**, like hardened tree sap. We can see every detail of its wings and how it flew.

First pterosaurs

Early birds

Bats appear

Biggest-ever birds

220 mya

155 mya

55 mya

6 mya

Triassic 251–200 mya	Jurassic 200–145 mya	Cretaceous 145–65 mya	Palaeogene 65–23 mya	Neogene 23–2.6 mya	Quaternary 2.6 mya–now

200 mya

100 mya

NOW

230 mya Early dinosaurs

65 mya Mass extinction kills off most land and many sea animals.

GLIDERS AND SWOOPERS

Some "flying" animals, like today's flying squirrels, are not true fliers. They cannot stay in the air for long, but are gliders that gradually swoop downward. Long ago, very different animals did this.

The lizardlike *Coelurosauravus* could glide well on large flaps of skin, one on either side of its body, held out by long thin bones. It probably did this to escape from enemies chasing it through the branches.

An even bigger reptile glider was *Kuehneosaurus*. With wing flaps as long as your arms, it drifted slowly downward as if wearing two parachutes.

WILD!

When scientists first found fossils of the thin wing bones of *Coelurosauravus*, they were puzzled. One idea was that the bones were from the long fins of a very different creature——a fish!

HOW BIG?

Coelurosauravus
15.8 inches (40 centimeters) long

◑ *Kuehneosaurus* was about 27.6 inches (70 centimeters) long and it lived at the same time as the early dinosaurs. Maybe it was gliding along and one of the meat-eating dinosaurs jumped up to catch and eat it.

◑ *Coelurosauravus* could not flap or beat its wings. But it could alter their shape to steer left or right, with the help of its long tail. These are its preserved fossils from more than 250 million years ago.

WILD FILE

Coelurosauravus

GROUP Reptiles

WHEN Late Permian Period

FOOD Small worms, bugs

FOSSIL SITES Western Europe, Madagascar

● Fossil sites

ON THE WING

To be a true flier, a creature must be able to stay in the air for many minutes, rise up and swoop down, and control where it goes. Could pterosaurs do this?

Yes, they could. **Pterosaurs** lived at the same time as the dinosaurs. The first ones could only flap weakly. Gradually, they became bigger, better, faster fliers, with powerful wing-beating muscles in their shoulders.

Dimorphodon probably flew over water to grab fish from the surface. It had a beaklike mouth filled with tiny sharp teeth to grip slippery **prey**.

WILD!

A pterosaur's wing was supported by the very long, thin bones of its fourth finger. It may have used its other fingers for grabbing prey from the sea's surface or from ledges along the cliffs.

HOW BIG?

Dimorphodon
Wingspan 4.6 feet (1. 4 meters)

The first pterosaurs, such as *Dimorphodon*, had a long trailing tail that probably helped them turn in the air. These creatures could walk and run on all fours, as well as fly.

WILD FILE

Dimorphodon

GROUP Tailed pterosaurs

WHEN Early Jurassic Period

FOOD Fish, insects, perhaps small animals such as lizards

WHERE Europe, North and Central America

Fossil sites

The fossils of *Eudimorphodon* show it had some long fanglike teeth, probably to bite wriggly victims such as fish. The 100 teeth behind them were smaller, but still very sharp.

STRANGE LOOKS

As dinosaurs took over the land, pterosaurs began to rule the skies. They became larger and stronger, and they hunted many kinds of creatures—especially fish.

Some pterosaurs had very strange body parts. Huge **Pteranodon** had a tall flap of bone on its head, called a head **crest**. This probably helped it steer and balance while flying.

Other pterosaurs had very long, slim beaks that curved up at the end and were filled with hundreds of thin, bendy teeth, like brush bristles. Perhaps they swished their beaks through the water to catch tiny creatures as food.

CLOSE COUSINS

The word "pterosaur" means winged lizard. But pterosaurs were much more closely related to crocodiles and to dinosaurs and birds than they were to lizards.

● With a body just 3.5 inches (9 centimeters) long, **Anurognathus** may have been the smallest pterosaur. Its large eyes were useful for finding insects, which it snapped up in its tiny, spiky teeth.

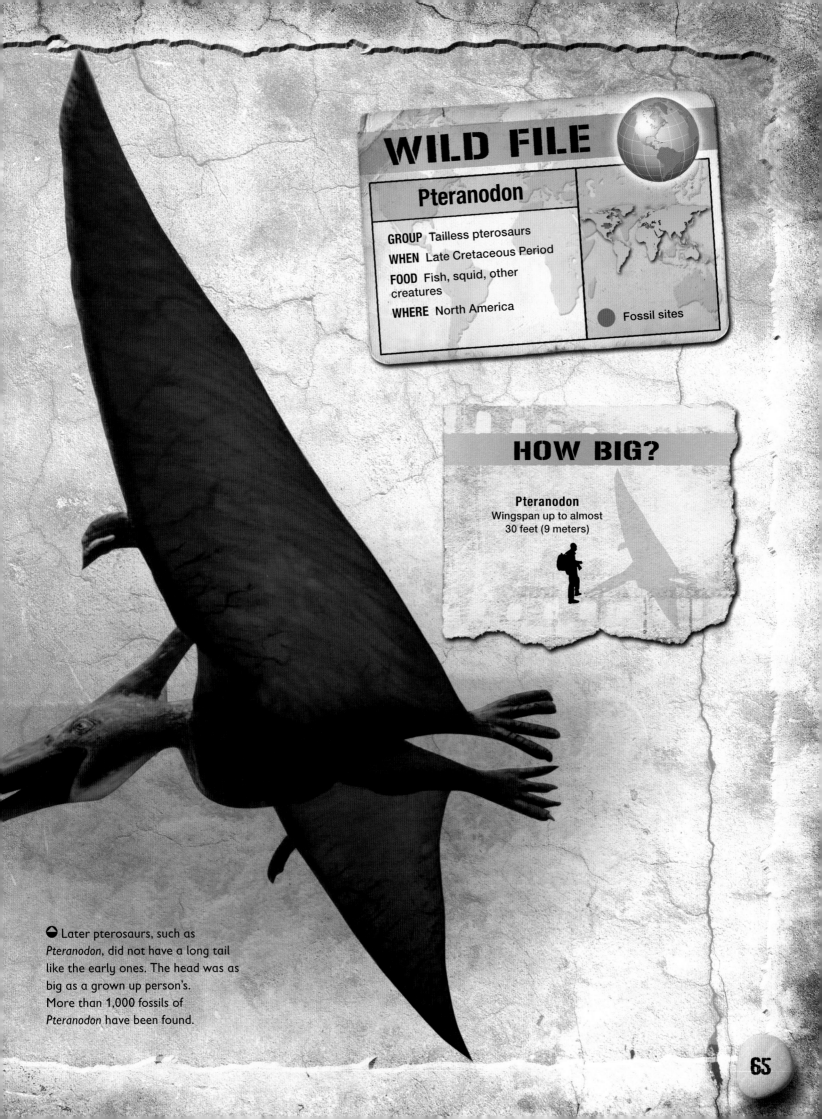

WILD FILE

Pteranodon

GROUP Tailless pterosaurs

WHEN Late Cretaceous Period

FOOD Fish, squid, other creatures

WHERE North America

Fossil sites

HOW BIG?

Pteranodon
Wingspan up to almost
30 feet (9 meters)

Later pterosaurs, such as *Pteranodon*, did not have a long tail like the early ones. The head was as big as a grown up person's. More than 1,000 fossils of *Pteranodon* have been found.

BIGGEST EVER FLIERS

Near the end of the Age of the Dinosaurs, pterosaurs became even more massive. Quetzalcoatlus was perhaps the biggest flying creature that ever lived.

Some experts thought that *Quetzalcoatlus* flew low over water to catch fish. Others suggested that it was a **scavenger**, pecking flesh from the dead bodies of dinosaurs and other animals. A newer idea is that *Quetzalcoatlus* walked on all fours, stabbing its victims such as baby dinosaurs.

Quetzalcoatlus and all other pterosaurs died out 65 million years ago, along with dinosaurs and many other kinds of creatures.

HOW BIG?

Quetzalcoatlus
Wingspan 39 feet (12 meters)

WILD!

Quetzalcoatlus could fold its wings back and up, and use its finger claws as front feet. With its back feet as well, it could run along the ground on its feet and claws faster than you can!

● *Ornithocherius* lived in what is now Brazil, South America. Its wings measured 20 feet (6 meters) from tip to tip—as long as a big car.

◐ *Quetzalcoatlus* may have soared over the mountains and plains like an enormous vulture, looking for dead animals to feast on.

WILD FILE

Quetzalcoatlus

GROUP Tailless pterosaurs

WHEN Late Cretaceous Period

FOOD Medium-sized animals such as baby dinosaurs

WHERE North America

● Fossil sites

EARLY BIRDS

In the middle of the Age of the Dinosaurs, some of the small meat-eating dinosaurs changed. They grew feathers, their arms turned to wings, and they became the first birds.

The earliest bird was *Archaeopteryx*. In many ways it was still similar to a small dinosaur. It had teeth in its beak, which no birds have today. It also had bones in its long tail, while modern birds have just feathers. *Archaeopteryx* also had finger claws on its wings, unlike today's birds.

Archaeopteryx was probably a good runner as well as a flier, and it may have hunted food on the ground.

WILD FILE

Archaeopteryx

GROUP Toothed birds

WHEN Late Jurassic Period

FOOD Bugs and small animals such as lizards

WHERE Europe

● Fossil sites

WILD!

Like all fossils, the fossil feathers of *Archaeopteryx* have no traces of their original colors. So, people who make pictures of this bird can color it any way they like!

◗ Take away the big, long feathers of *Archaeopteryx* and it would look very similar to a little dinosaur with small feathers, like this *Protarchaeopteryx*.

◗ *Archaeopteryx* spreads its wings, ready for takeoff. It was probably not an expert flier, like modern birds, but it could swoop and glide quite well.

HOW BIG?

Archaeopteryx
Wingspan 23.6 inches
(60 centimeters)

BIRDS TAKE OFF

Toward the end of the Age of the Dinosaurs, many new kinds of birds appeared in the skies. Some were as small as sparrows, while others were much larger— even bigger than us.

Confuciusornis was one of the bigger birds of the time, about the size of today's crow. Its many fossils show that *Confuciusornis* formed big groups, or flocks, that probably fed and rested together.

Eoalulavis was much smaller, hardly the size of a sparrow. Its wing shape was suited to very controlled flying, especially when taking off or landing. Birds were truly becoming expert fliers.

◗ *Confuciusornis* fossils come from China and are about 120 million years old. This was the first bird to have a real beak, rather than dinosaur-like jaws and teeth.

WILD FILE

Confuciusornis

GROUP Birds

WHEN Early Cretaceous Period

FOOD Seeds, perhaps small animals

WHERE China

● Fossil sites

HOW BIG?

Confuciusornis
Wingpsan 35.4 inches
(90 centimeters)

WILD!

Fossils of *Confuciusornis* show two kinds, one with very long tail feathers and one with a much shorter tail. Maybe these were male and female, like some modern birds such as pheasants.

● ***Caudipteryx*** was about as big as a peacock. It had long feathers on its arms and tail. Yet it was not a bird—it was a dinosaur. Its wings were far too small and weak for flight.

WINGS OVER WATER

The first birds probably fed on the ground or in tree branches. Then, some kinds started to feed in water, catching fish and other prey. They became swimmers, as well as fliers.

Dasornis was a type of goose, but far bigger than any geese today. It could probably land on water and swim along by kicking with its feet.

When *Dasornis* was hungry, it took off and swooped over the surface to catch slippery fish. It grabbed them using the rows of tiny teeth in its massive beak.

HOW BIG?

Dasornis
Wingspan 16.4 feet (5 meters)

◐ *Dasornis* had very long, thin wings, like an albatross. This shape is good for gliding long distances without making much effort.

WILD FILE

Dasornis

GROUP Wildfowl birds

WHEN Early Paleogene Period

FOOD Fish, squid, other sea creatures

WHERE Europe

● Fossil sites

◑ *Presbyornis* was a tall shorebird with long legs, about 3 feet (1 meter) high. It lived after the Age of the Dinosaurs, around 60–40 million years ago, in North America.

TO FLY OR NOT?

Today, most birds are expert fliers. But some, such as ostriches and penguins, cannot fly at all. Long ago there were also flightless birds.

Hesperornis was a seabird that lost the power of flight and turned into an expert swimmer. Its wings were tiny, but its legs had big paddle-shaped feet for moving very fast through the water. *Hesperornis* chased fish and similar food under the surface.

Like *Hesperornis*, **Ichthyornis** had teeth in its beak and probably ate fish. But it caught them while flying, by swooping down to just under the water's surface, then taking off again.

HOW BIG?

Hesperornis
6.5 feet (2 meters)
high

WILD!

When *Hesperornis* fossils were first discovered over a hundred years ago, experts thought they were the remains of a fierce lizard that swam in the sea!

WILD FILE

Hesperornis

GROUP Seabirds
WHEN Late Cretaceous Period
FOOD Fish, other water creatures
WHERE North America, including Canada

● Fossil sites

● *Ichthyornis* was the Dinosaur Age version of our modern seagulls and terns. It was about gull-sized and its fossils suggest it had strong wings and flying muscles.

● *Hesperornis* was a big, heavy bird that could only waddle on land. It may have been hunted by hungry dinosaurs prowling along the shore.

BIG COUSINS

Long ago, the birds that flew in the skies were close relatives of birds alive today. Some of those distant relations were giants!

The largest-ever eagle was *Harpagornis*, or Haast's eagle, from New Zealand. Its prey included the flightless birds known as **moas**. Both the eagle and the moas died out—but only about 1,400 years ago.

The biggest penguin today is the emperor penguin, at 47 inches (120 centimeters) tall. About 40 million years ago, the giant penguin **Anthropornis** was 15.8 inches (40 centimeters) taller—as high as an adult person!

WILD!

Harpagornis lived at the same time as early people. It was such a strong and powerful animal that *Harpagornis* may have even carried away human babies and young children.

HOW BIG?

Harpagornis
Wingspan 10.5 feet
(3.2 meters)

◑ The giant penguin *Anthropornis* lived about 40 million years ago. It probably hunted fish and squid in the sea and rested on land, like today's penguins.

◑ *Harpargonis* swooped down to carry off its prey, mostly newborn and young flightless birds. It had huge claws, or talons, to stab into its victims and a sharp hooked beak to tear their flesh apart.

WILD FILE

Harpagornis

GROUP Birds of prey
WHEN Until 1,400 years ago
FOOD Large birds and
ground animals
WHERE New Zealand

New Zealand

● Fossil sites

SHADOWS IN THE SKY

Giant birds of prey once cast a shadow over the land. There were also fearsome hunting birds that could not fly—but they could outrun most other animals.

WILD FILE

Argentavis

GROUP Birds of prey
WHEN Late Neogene Period
FOOD Sick or dead animals
WHERE South America

● Fossil sites

Argentavis was the biggest flying bird of all time. Its wings were twice as long as the albatross, the bird with the longest wings now. Its sharp beak shows that it probably scavenged, eating dying or dead creatures.

Titanis was flightless, like today's ostrich, but much stronger and heavier. It ran after victims on its powerful legs and tore them apart with its fierce hooked beak.

WILD!

Argentavis was so big and heavy that, to take off, it probably jumped from a cliff or ran downhill into the wind. Once in the air, it could glide for hours without flapping its huge wings.

HOW BIG?

Argentavis
Wingspan 23 feet (7 meters)

◖ We don't know if *Argentavis* had a bare head and neck, like today's vultures. If so, it would not have had feathers to get covered in blood as it pecked inside dead animals.

◗ *Titanis* was as tall as a doorway. This top predator could even catch and tear apart the small horses that lived in the Neogene Period.

NIGHT FLIERS

As birds took over the skies during the daytime, other creatures began to hunt in the dark. They were furry mammals whose arms became long wings—the bats.

The first known bat was *Icaronycteris*, from 50–40 million years ago. It looked very similar to bats of today, with wings of leathery skin held out by long finger bones.

Icaronycteris found its way in the dark like today's bats. It made squeaks and listened to the echoes bouncing back off nearby objects. We know this from the small, delicate fossils of its ear and mouth bones.

HOW BIG?

Icaronycteris
Wingspan 13.8–15.8 inches (35–40 centimeters)

◖ *Icaronycteris* caught small flying creatures, such as moths and flies, with its sharp teeth. It could hang upside down by its feet, just like modern bats.

Icaronycteris

GROUP Bats (mammals)

WHEN Early–Mid Paleogene Period

FOOD Moths, similar flying insects

WHERE North America

● Fossil sites

● Fossils of the bat *Palaeochiropteryx* come from Germany. They look very jumbled here, but the long arm bones and thin finger bones can be seen.

CLOSE COUSINS

Bats did not develop, or **evolve**, from feathery birds. They probably evolved from small, furry tree-living **mammals**, which were similar to today's tree shrews.

KEEP WARM WITH
WOOLLY MAMMOTHS...

SHELTER FROM THE COLD
WITH CAVE CREATURES...

MEET THE
FIRST HUMANS...

MANY ICE AGES

Have you been to a cold, snowy, icy place? Imagine living there all the time. You would be freezing! That's what huge parts of our world were like long, long ago—yet animals survived.

Today, there is plenty of snow and ice around the North and South Poles. In a real Ice Age, much larger areas of the Earth were frozen over for thousands or even millions of years. This has happened many times since the Earth began.

One of the coldest times was the Andean-Saharan Ice Age, which started about 460 million years ago. Up to half the world was frozen for more than 20 million years. It was the time of **Snowball Earth**. Even in the warmer places, creatures and plants struggled to survive.

Andean-Saharan Ice Age **460–430 mya**

Karoo Ice Age **350–270 mya**

Ediacaran	Cambrian	Ordovician	Silurian	Devonian	Carboniferous	Permian
before 542 mya	542–488 mya	488–444 mya	444–416 mya	416–359 mya	359–299 mya	299–251 mya

550 mya 500 mya 400 mya 300 mya

540 mya 460 mya 430 mya 360 mya

Shelled sea animals Land plants Tiny land animals Four-legged land animals

⬤ Sea scorpions, or *eurypterids*, were fierce hunters in the seas from 450 to 250 million years ago. As the seas cooled, they became less common.

⬤ Throughout the huge length of prehistoric time, the last Ice Ages were fairly recent. They took place in the Quaternary Period and ended only 10,000 years ago.

⬤ These are fossils of *Diictodon*, a creature midway between a reptile and a mammal, that lived 255 million years ago. It thrived during warm times, but died out as the world became colder.

10,000 years ago—last Ice Age ends
20,000 years ago—peak of last Ice Age
150,000 years ago—woolly mammoths appear

Polar regions ice over
20 mya

Recent Ice Ages begin
2.6 mya

Neogene | Quaternary

Triassic 251–200 mya	Jurassic 200–145 mya	Cretaceous 145–65 mya	Palaeogene 65–23 mya	Neogene 23–2.6 mya	Quaternary 2.6 mya–now

200 mya — 100 mya — NOW

230 mya

Early dinosaurs

65 mya

Mass extinction kills off most land and many sea animals.

RECENT ICE AGES

A series of about 20 Ice Ages began 2.5 million years ago. The last one finished only around 10,000 years ago.

During each of these Ice Ages, ice spread over much of the land and the sea in the northern half of the world, and over large areas of the southern half. After 40,000 years or more, a warmer period followed and most of the ice melted away.

Animals that were very different from those alive today lived during the Ice Ages. *Homotherium,* the scimitar cat, used its swordlike curved front teeth to slice up its victims, such as deer.

WILD!

In just one cave in Texas, the remains of more than 30 *Homotherium* were found. The cave also contained remains of their food—more than 300 young mammoths!

WILD FILE

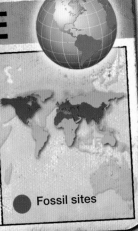

Homotherium

GROUP Mammals— cats

WHEN Five million to 10,000 years ago

FOOD Deer, wild cattle, elephants, mammoths, rhinos, horses

FOSSIL SITES Most northern lands, also North Africa

● Fossil sites

At the peak of the most recent Ice Age, much of North America and Northern Europe was completely covered by a thick sheet of ice. The lands to the south were much colder than they are today.

Homotherium may have hunted in groups to catch prey such as wild horses. The fierce cats clawed, jabbed, and stabbed the victim so it bled to death.

The World 20,000 Years Ago

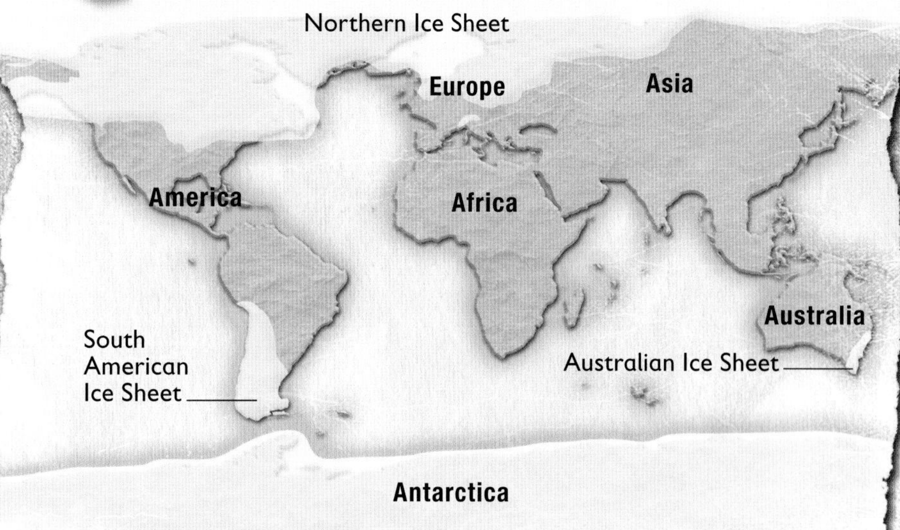

Northern Ice Sheet

Europe

Asia

America

Africa

Australia

South American Ice Sheet

Australian Ice Sheet

Antarctica

HOW BIG?

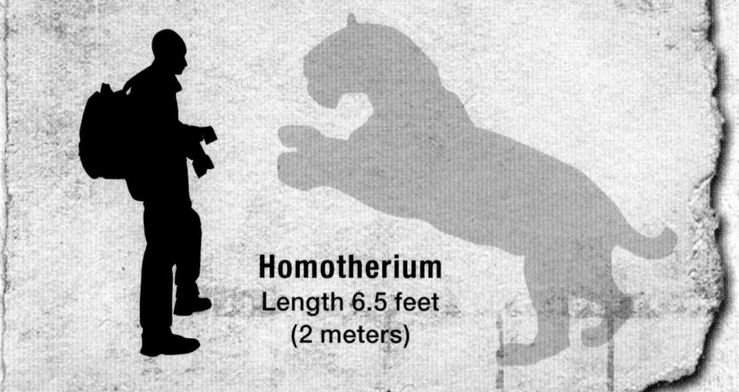

Homotherium
Length 6.5 feet
(2 meters)

KEEPING WARM

To keep warm in cold weather, you put on a coat. Some Ice Age animals grew their own warm coats—made of long fur or hair.

Only the animals called mammals have furry or woolly coats. One of the thickest coats belonged to the woolly **mammoth**, a type of elephant. Some of its hairs were more than 3 feet (1 meter) long. The woolly mammoth also had long, curving **tusks** to scrape away snow and reach its plant food.

The woolly rhinoceros also had a thick fur coat. Its front **nose horn** was more than 3 feet (1 meter) long.

WILD!

Woolly mammoths have been found deep-frozen in the ice of the far north. One, called "Baby Lubya," was just one month old when she died 40,000 years ago, in the far north of what is now Russia.

● The woolly rhinoceros had two nose horns. It lived across the north of Europe and Asia. It was even larger than the biggest rhinoceros of today, the white rhino of Africa.

WILD FILE

Woolly mammoth

GROUP Mammals—elephants

WHEN 150,000 to 4,000 years ago

FOOD Grasses, leaves, roots

FOSSIL SITES Northern parts of North America, Europe, and Asia

● Fossil sites

● The tusks of the woolly mammoth reached 16 feet (5 meters) in length. This mammoth had a lumpy top to the head and a big shoulder hump, but quite small ears.

HOW BIG?

Woolly mammoth
11.5 feet (3.5 meters) to the shoulder

CAVE DANGERS

When a freezing wind brings lots of snow, a cave offers welcome shelter. But during the Ice Age, many caves had huge fierce animals inside!

The cave bear was a massive cousin of today's grizzly bear. It probably stayed in its cave through the long winter, in a deep sleep called **hibernation**. In the summer, it wandered the grasslands and woods, searching for all kinds of food.

Other Ice Age creatures that sheltered in caves included cave lions and cave hyenas. Some Ice Age caves were very crowded!

WILD!

Some caves contain the remains of more than 100 bears. They may have all died together during an extra cold winter. There were also bones of their prey, such as deer.

WILD FILE

Cave bear

GROUP Mammals—bears

WHEN One million to 27,000 years ago

FOOD Most foods—plant and animal

FOSSIL SITE Western and Northern Europe

● Fossil sites

HOW BIG?

Cave bear
10 feet (3 meters)
long

⬭ After months in their shelter, a mother cave bear and her young cubs look out at the spring sunshine. They are very hungry, and it's time to go outside for fresh air and food.

⬭ Cave paintings by ancient humans show that the cave lion probably had faint stripes, like a tiger. It hunted all kinds of creatures, including caribou (reindeer).

MASSIVE PLANT-EATERS

Some Ice Age animals roamed the snowy grasslands, while others wandered in the woods and forests. The giant deer probably did both.

The giant deer's body was only slightly bigger than that of the largest deer today, the moose. But its **antlers** were far bigger. They measured more than 11.5 feet (3.5 meters) across and were very heavy—they weighed more than you!

As with most deer, only the males grew antlers. They probably used their antlers to fight each other at **breeding time**, to take control of the herd of females.

WILD FILE

Giant deer

GROUP Mammals—deer

WHEN 400,000 to 8,000 years ago

FOOD Grasses, leaves, shoots, fruit

FOSSIL SITES Northern parts of Europe and Asia

● Fossil sites

HOW BIG?

Giant deer
7.2 feet (2.2 meters)

⬤ The giant deer is sometimes called the "Irish elk" because many of its remains are found in peat bogs in Ireland. But it also lived in many other places across Europe and Asia.

⬤ *Toxodon* lived in South America during the recent Ice Ages. It looked like a mixture of rhinoceros and hippopotamus, and it fed on grasses and low-growing shrubs.

93

HUNTERS, HUNTED

There were many hunting animals during the Ice Ages, including fierce wolves and powerful big cats.

The dire wolf was one of the main Ice Age predators. It probably hunted in groups called packs.

What did these wolves eat? We know about Ice Age animals from their fossils, which are the remains of once-living things preserved in the rocks and turned to stone. Fossils of dire wolves have been found with fossils of their victims, which have ranged from horses and deer to camels, elephants, and even giant beavers!

⬤ As well as being a hunter, the dire wolf may have been a scavenger. Its strong jaws and teeth could crunch up the bits of dead animals left by other predators, such as **saber-toothed cats**.

HOW BIG?

Dire wolf
6.5 feet (2 meters)
nose-to-tail

Dire wolf

GROUP Mammals—carnivores

WHEN 1.8 million to 11,000 years ago

FOOD Many creatures, from mice to elephants

FOSSIL SITES North and South America

● Fossil sites

CLOSE COUSINS

The dire wolf was bigger than today's gray wolf and had longer, stronger legs. Once the dire wolf pack started chasing a victim, there was no escape!

● *Hipparion* was a small type of horse that lived in America during the early Ice Ages of recent times. It was attacked by many predators, including dire wolves and the huge, fierce, flightless bird *Titanis*.

AWAY FROM THE ICE

Even during the coldest Ice Ages, some parts of the world stayed fairly warm. Yet more strange giant creatures lived here.

While northern areas were gripped by ice, the middle of the world—called the tropics—and some southern areas were ice-free. One of the biggest animals here was the giant ground sloth.

As huge as an elephant, the giant ground sloth *Megatherium* had long, sharp claws to dig up plant food. It also used these fearsome claws to defend itself against enemies, such as dire wolves and saber-toothed cats.

HOW BIG?

Giant ground sloth
20 feet (6 meters) high

🔴 *Hippidion* was a pony-sized horse that lived in South America at the same time as the giant ground sloth. It died out around 8,000 years ago, perhaps hunted to extinction by people.

WILD FILE

Giant ground sloth

GROUP Mammals— sloths and armadillos

WHEN Five million to 10,000 years ago

FOOD Plants

FOSSIL SITES Central and South America

● Fossil sites

WILD!

Megatherium's tongue may have been more than 3 feet (1 meter) long! The giant ground sloth could probably rear up and run on its two back legs with a kind of very fast waddle.

◗ Megatherium probably stood on its two rear legs and leaned back on its strong tail to reach the leaves high up in trees. It could pull branches to its mouth with its big front claws.

DWARFS AND PYGMIES

Many Ice Age animals were much bigger than their relatives of today. Yet some were much smaller!

During the Ice Ages there were dwarf or "pygmy" kinds of many animals. Most lived on small islands where there was limited food. The pygmy mammoth of islands off western North America was probably not much taller than you. It weighed less than one-tenth of its giant cousin on mainland America, the Columbian mammoth.

There were also mini-versions of woolly mammoths, elephants, camels, rhinos, and horses.

HOW BIG?

Pygmy mammoth
5 feet (1.5 meters)
to shoulder

◑ There were several kinds of *Teleoceras*, a rhinoceros with short legs and a small horn. The dwarf kind lived in swampy areas, wading and swimming like a hippopotamus.

Pygmy mammoths probably descended from the much larger Columbian mammoth. They lived on the Channel Islands, off the coast of what is now California.

WILD FILE

Pygmy mammoth

GROUP Mammals—elephants

WHEN One million to 11,000 years ago

FOOD Grasses, leaves

FOSSIL SITES Western North America

● Fossil sites

WILD!

The dwarf woolly mammoths of Wrangel Island, off Northeast Asia, survived until less than 4,000 years ago. The island is small and very cold and snowy for most of the year, with little food.

AMAZING AUSTRALIA

Australia, in the south of the world, did not freeze much during the Ice Ages. But it was far colder than today, and some of its animals grew to huge sizes.

The giant wombat was the biggest-ever pouched animal, or **marsupial**. It roamed the plains and woods of Australia, feeding on all kinds of plants.

The giant wombat was so massive that it had few enemies. Perhaps a very hungry marsupial lion might attack it. Or a big eagle could swoop down to carry off its baby.

WILD FILE

Giant wombat

GROUP Mammals—marsupials

WHEN 1.6 million to 40,000 years ago

FOOD Plants

FOSSIL SITES Australia

Fossil sites

HOW BIG?

Giant wombat
Length 10 feet (3 meters) nose-to-tail

The marsupial lion was smaller than the African lions of today. But it was very strong with an extremely powerful bite, and could probably kill a giant kangaroo.

The giant wombat looked similar to its living cousin, the hairy-nosed wombat, but with a bigger head and snout. Like other marsupials, it carried its baby in a pouch. Many of these wombats died of thirst in **droughts**.

DEADLY CATS

Many kinds of big cats hunted during the Ice Ages. Some had teeth that were longer than carving knives, and just as sharp!

Smilodon was a saber-toothed cat from North and South America. It had a short tail, but very strong legs and paws for catching big **prey**.

Smilodon's two main front teeth were up to 12 inches (30 centimeters) long. They were very sharp, but quite thin. *Smilodon* probably used them to stab into its victim, or to slash its flesh and cause gaping wounds so the prey bled to death.

WILD FILE

Smilodon

GROUP Mammals—cats

WHEN 1.5 million to 10,000 years ago

FOOD Other animals, from rats to elephants

FOSSIL SITES North and South America

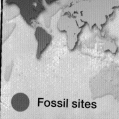 Fossil sites

◖ *Megantereon* was one of the most widespread of saber-toothed cats. Its fossils have been found all around the north of the world and in Africa—where it chased antelopes and gazelles.

CLOSE COUSINS

The American giant lion of the Ice Ages was even larger than today's African lion. It was almost as big and heavy as the largest type of *Smilodon*, which was called *Smilodon populator*.

◖ *Smilodon* could open its mouth very wide, ready to strike its prey as though cutting it with a big knife. It may have gone for the throat —to cut the blood vessels and breathing tube.

HOW BIG?

Smilodon
7.2 feet (2.2 meters) nose-to-tail

MAMMOTH SIZE

There are no mammoths alive today. But during the Ice Ages, several kinds of these huge beasts roamed various parts of the world.

One of the biggest was the Columbian mammoth. It was twice as heavy as most living elephants. Almost as massive was its close cousin, the American **mastodon**.

Many mammoths and mastodons have been preserved in natural **tar pits**. Other plant-eaters died here, too, such as ground sloths, giant buffalo, camels, deer, and horses. Hunters were also killed, including dire wolves, saber-toothed cats, and American lions and cheetahs.

WILD FILE

Columbian mammoth

GROUP Mammals—elephants

WHEN 250,000 to 8,000 years ago

FOOD Grasses, fruits, and other plant parts

FOSSIL SITES North and Central America

Fossil sites

HOW BIG?

Columbian mammoth
13 feet (4 meters) to the shoulder

WILD!

The Columbian mammoth's curving tusks stretched as long as a family car! The great beast probably used them to dig up roots, to snap branches off trees, and to fight its enemies.

◑ A mammoth's tusks grew gradually over the years, so the oldest mammoths had the longest tusks. The Columbian mammoth probably lived to the age of 70 or 80 years.

◐ The American mastodon was a close cousin of the elephants and mammoths. It probably fed on leaves from trees and bushes.

ICE AGE PEOPLE

During the Ice Ages, it wasn't just animals that braved the freezing winds and thick snow. There were also human beings—people a lot like us.

Two kinds of humans lived during the recent Ice Ages. First were the Neanderthal people. They made stone tools such as scrapers and spears, built shelters, lit fires, and made clothes from animal furs to keep warm.

Neanderthals died out 30,000 years ago. As the Ice Age began to fade, another type of human, called **Homo sapiens**, spread more widely. These were modern humans—just like you.

WILD!

Neanderthal people probably used blazing torches to drive mammoths over cliffs or into pits. Then, they ate the mammoth meat, wore their furry skin, and carved their tusks into tools.

◓ More than 15,000 years ago, people drew pictures of animals in caves, such as this early horse. These pictures show us what many **extinct** animals looked like.

WILD FILE

Neanderthal human

GROUP Mammal— primates

WHEN 250,000 to 32,000 years ago

FOOD Many foods, from nuts and berries to mammoth meat

FOSSIL SITES Europe and West Asia

● Fossil sites

HOW BIG?

Neanderthal human
5.4 feet
(1.65 meters)

❶ Neanderthal people looked very similar to us. But they were stronger, with more powerful muscles, wider noses, longer bodies, and shorter legs. They used many kinds of tools to kill and cut up the animals they hunted.

WILD GUIDE

Acanthostega

Pronunciation ack-an-tho-stay-ga
Meaning Spiky roof
Group Tetrapods
Time Late Devonian, 365 mya
Length 23.6 in (60 cm)
Weight 11 lb (5 kg)

Ambulocetus

Pronunciation am-byoo-low-seet-us
Meaning Walking whale
Group Whales and dolphins (cetaceans)
Time period Early Paleogene, 50 mya
Size 9.8 ft (3 m)
Weight 440 lb (200 kg)

Andrewsarchus

Pronunciation an-drew-sark-us
Meaning Andrew's ruler
Group Mammals—mesonychid
Time Paleogene, 40 mya
Length 14.8 ft (4.5 m)
Weight 1543 lb (700 kg)

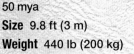

Anomalocaris

Pronunciation an-om-uh-lowe-carr-is
Meaning Strange shrimp
Group Crabs and shrimps (crustaceans)
Time period Cambrian, 500 mya
Size Up to 3.3 ft. (1 m) long
Weight About 18 lbs. (8 kg)

Anthropornis

Pronunciation an-throw-por-nis
Meaning Human-like bird
Group Penguins
Time Mid Palaeogene, 40 mya
Wingspan 3.6 ft (1.1 m)
Height 5.3 ft (1.6 m)

Anurognathus

Pronunciation ann-your-og-nay-thus
Meaning Without tail jaw
Group Tailed pterosaurs
Time Late Jurassic, 150 mya
Wingspan 20 in (50 cm)
Length 3.5 in (9 cm)

Archaeopteryx

Pronunciation ark-ee-op-tur-ix
Meaning Ancient wing
Group Toothed birds
Time Late Jurassic, 150 mya
Wingspan 23.6 in (60 cm)
Length 20 in (50 cm)

Archelon

Pronunciation ark-ee-lon
Meaning Ruler turtle
Group Turtles (chelonians)
Time period Late Cretaceous, 70 mya
Size 13 ft (4 m) long
Weight About 2 tons

Argentavis

Pronunciation
are-jen-tay-viss

Meaning Magnificent
Argentine bird

Group Birds of prey

Time Late Neogene, 5 mya

Wingspan 23 ft (7 m)

Length 11.5 ft (3.5 m)

Arthropleura

Pronunciation
are-throw-plur-a

Meaning Rib joint

Group Arthropods

Time Mid Carboniferous,
340–300 mya

Length 8.2 ft (2.5 m)

Weight 220 lb (100 kg)

Basilosaurus

Pronunciation
baz-ill-oh-saw-rus

Meaning Emperor lizard

Group Whales and dolphins
(cetaceans)

Time period Mid Paleogene,
35 mya

Size 82 ft (25 m)

Weight 66 tons

Bothriolepis

Pronunciation
both-ree-oh-lep-iss

Meaning Pitted scale

Group Armored fish
(placoderms)

Time period Devonian, 370
mya

Size 11.8 in (30 cm) long

Weight 2.2 lb (1 kg)

Canis dirus
(Dire wolf)

Pronunciation
kan-iss die-rus

Meaning Dreadful wolf

Group Mammals—wolves

Time Quaternary, 1.8 million to
10,000 ya

Length 6.5 ft (2 m)

Weight 176 lb (80 kg)

Caudipteryx

Pronunciation
caw-dip-tur-ix

Meaning Tail feather

Group Dinosaurs

Time Early Cretaceous, 125
mya

Weight 6.6 lb (3 kg)

Length 3.3 ft (1 m)

Cephalaspis

Pronunciation
seff-al-ass-pis

Meaning Head shield

Group Jawless fish
(agnathans)

Time period Devonian, 400
mya

Size 20 in (50 cm) long

Weight About 4 lb (2 kg)

Climatius

Pronunciation
kly-mate-ee-us

Meaning Zone fish

Group Spiny sharks
(acanthodians)

Time period Silurian-Devonian,
420–410 mya

Size 3.2 in (8 cm) long

Weight 8.8 oz (250 g)

Coelacanth

Pronunciation
seel-uh-kanth

Meaning Hollow spine

Group Lobe-finned fish
(sarcopterygians)

Time period Devonian, 400
mya, to today

Size 6.5 ft (2 m) long

Weight 176 lb (80 kg)

Coelodonta
(Woolly rhino)

Pronunciation
seel-oh-don-ta

Meaning Chamber tooth

Group Mammals—rhinos

Time Quaternary, 100,000 to
10,000 ya

Length 14 ft (4.4 m)

Weight 2 tons

Coelurosauravus

Pronunciation
seel-ure-oh-saw-rave-us
Meaning Hollow reptile bird
Group Reptiles
Time Late Permian, 255 mya
Wingspan 11 in (30 cm)
Length 15 in (40 cm)

Confuciusornis

Pronunciation
con-few-she-us-orn-iss
Meaning Confucius bird
Group Beaked birds
Time Early-Mid Cretaceous, 120 mya
Wingspan 33 in (90 cm)
Length 11 in (30 cm)

Cynognathus

Pronunciation
sigh-nog-nay-thus
Meaning Dog jaw
Group Mammal-like reptiles
Time Early Triassic, 240 mya
Length 3 ft (1 m)
Weight 66 lb (30 kg)

Dasornis

Pronunciation
das-orn-iss
Meaning Hairy bird
Group Wildfowl birds
Time Early Palaeogene, 50 mya
Wingspan 16 ft (5 m)
Length 3 ft (1 m)

Desmatosuchus

Pronunciation
dez-mat-oh-sook-us
Meaning Link crocodile
Group Reptiles – aetosaurs
Time Late Triassic, 210 mya
Length 16 ft (5 m)
Weight 880 lb (400 kg)

Diadectes

Pronunciation
die-uh-deck-teez
Meaning Royal swimmer
Group Tetrapods – amphibian-like
Time Early Permian, 280 mya
Length 10 ft. (3 m)
Weight 330 lb (150 kg)

Diictodon

Pronunciation
die-ick-toe-don
Meaning Two teeth
Group Therapsids or Mammal-like reptiles
Time Late Permian, 255 mya
Length 23 in (60 cm)
Weight 6.6 lb (3 kg)

Dimetrodon

Pronunciation *die-meet-row-don*
Meaning Two measures of teeth
Group Tetrapods – pelycosaurs
Time Mid Permian, 275 mya
Length 11 ft (3.5 m)
Weight 330 lb (150 kg)

Dimorphodon

Pronunciation
die-mor-foe-don
Meaning Two forms of teeth
Group Tailed pterosaurs
Time Early Jurassic, 190 mya
Wingspan 4.5 ft (1.4 m)
Length 3 ft (1 m)

Diprotodon
(Giant wombat)

Pronunciation
dip-roe-toe-don
Meaning Two front teeth
Group Mammals – marsupials
Time Quaternary, 1.6 to 40,000 ya
Length 10 ft (3 m)
Weight 2 tons

Doedicurus

Pronunciation
Doe-ed-i-cure-us
Meaning Pestle or hammer tail
Group Mammals – sloths and armadillos
Time Quaternary, 1.5 million to 12,000 ya
Length 13 ft (4 m)
Weight 2 tons

Dunkleosteus

Pronunciation
dunk-lee-oss-tee-us
Meaning Dunkle's bone
Group Armored fish (placoderms)
Time period Late Devonian, 370 mya
Size 33 ft (10 m) long
Weight More than 3 tons

Elasmosaurus

Pronunciation
ee-laz-mow-saw-rus
Meaning Thin plate
Group Plesiosaurs
Time period Late Cretaceous, 70 mya
Size 46 ft (14 m) long
Weight 2 tons

Elasmotherium

Pronunciation
ee-laz-mow-theer-ee-um
Meaning Thin plate beast
Group Mammals – rhinos
Time Quaternary, 2.5 million to 130,000 ya
Length 20 ft (6 m)
Weight 7 tons

Eryops

Pronunciation
air-ee-ops
Meaning Long face
Group Tetrapods – amphibian-like
Time Early Permian, 295 mya
Length 6.5 ft (2 m)
Weight 175 lb (80 kg)

Estemmenosuchus

Pronunciation
es-tem-en-oh-sook-us
Meaning Crowned crocodile
Group Mammal-like reptiles
Time Late Permian, 260 mya
Length 13 ft (4 m)
Weight 1,750 lb (800 kg)

Eudimorphodon

Pronunciation
you-dee-mor-foe-don
Meaning Truly two forms of teeth
Group Tailed pterosaurs
Time Late Triassic, 205 mya
Wingspan 37.5 in (100 cm)
Length 37.5 in (100 cm)

Gastornis

Pronunciation
gass-torn-iss
Meaning Gaston's bird
Group Birds – flightless
Time Palaeogene, 50 mya
Height 6 ft (2 m)
Weight 330 lb (150 kg)

Harpagornis

Pronunciation
harp-ah-gorn-iss
Meaning Hook-beaked bird
Group Birds of prey
Time Quaternary, until 1400 ya
Wingspan 10 ft (3 m)
Length 4 ft (1.2 m)

Hipparion

Pronunciation
hih-par-ee-on
Meaning Pony
Group Mammals – horses
Time Neogene to Quaternary, 12 million to 750,000 ya
Height 4.6 ft (1.4 m)
Weight 220 lb (100 kg)

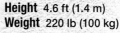

Hippidion

Pronunciation
hih-pid-ee-on
Meaning Little horse
Group Mammals—horses
Time Quaternary, 2 million to 8,000 ya
Height 4.6 ft (1.4 m)
Weight 660 lb (300 kg)

Homo neanderthalensis (Neanderthal human)

Pronunciation
Hoe-moe nee-an-dur-taal-en-sis
Meaning Person from Neander Valley
Group Mammals—primates
When Quaternary, 250,000 to 32,000 years ago
Height 5.4 ft (1.65 m)
Weight 200 lb (90 kg)

Homo sapiens (Modern human)

Pronunciation
hoe-moe say-pee-ens
Meaning Wise person
Group Mammals—primates
Time Quaternary, 200,000 ya until now
Height 5.4 ft (1.65 m)
Weight 165 lb (75 kg)

Homotherium

Pronunciation
hoe-moe-theer-ee-um
Meaning Man-eating beast
Group Mammals—cats
Time Neogene to Quaternary, 5 million to 10,000 ya
Length 6.5 ft (2 m)
Weight 400 lb (180 kg)

Hyaenodon

Pronunciation
high-een-oh-don
Meaning Hyaena tooth
Group Mammals—creodonts
Time Paleogene–Neogene, 40–20 mya
Length 9.8 ft (9 m)
Weight 440 lb (200 kg)

Icaronycteris

Pronunciation
ik-are-oh-nick-tur-iss
Meaning Icarus night creature
Group Bats
Time Early-Mid Paleogene, 50–40 mya
Wingspan 13.8–15.8 in (35–40 cm)
Length 6 in (15 cm)

Ichthyornis

Pronunciation
ick-thee-or-niss
Meaning Fish bird
Group Prehistoric seabirds
Time Late Cretaceous, 90–75 mya
Wingspan 23.6 in (60 cm)
Length 11.8 in (30 cm)

Ichthyosaurus

Pronunciation
ick-thee-oh-saw-rus
Meaning Fish lizard
Group Ichthyosaurs
Time period Early Jurassic, 190 mya
Size 6.5 ft (2 m) long
Weight 165 lb (75 kg)

Ichthyostega

Pronunciation
ick-thee-oh-stay-ga
Meaning Fish roof
Group Tetrapods
Time Late Devonian, 365 mya
Length 5 ft (1.5 m)
Weight 55 lb (25 kg)

Kronosaurus

Pronunciation
crow-no-saw-rus
Meaning Time lizard
Group Pliosaurs (short-necked plesiosaurs)
Time period Early Cretaceous, 110 mya
Size 3.3 ft (10 m) long
Weight 10 tons

Kuehneosaurus

Pronunciation
koo-enn-ee-oh-saw-rus
Meaning Kuehn's lizard
Group Reptiles
Time Late Triassic, 200 mya
Wingspan 15.8 in (40 cm)
Length 27.6 in (70 cm)

Mammut americanum (American mastodon)

Pronunciation
mamm-oot ah-mare-ick-arn-um
Meaning Mastodon of America
Group Mammals—elephants
Time Neogene and Quaternary, 3.7 million to 10,000 ya
Height 10 ft (3 m)
Weight 7 tons

Mammuthus columbi (Columbian mammoth)

Pronunciation
mam-oo-thus ko-lum-bee
Meaning Mammoth of Columbia
Group Mammals—elephants
Time Quaternary, 250,000 to 8,000 ya
Height 13 ft (4 m)
Weight 11 tons

Mammuthus exilis (Pygmy mammoth)

Pronunciation
mam-oo-thus ex-ill-iss
Meaning Removed mammoth
Group Mammals—elephants
When Neogene Period, 1 million to 11,000 ya
Height 5 ft (1.5 m)
Weight 2,000 lb (900 kg)

Mammuthus primigenius (Woolly mammoth)

Pronunciation
mam-oo-thus prim-ee-geen-ee-us
Meaning First-made mammoth
Group Mammals—elephants
Time Quaternary, 150,000 to less than 4000 ya
Length 23 ft (7 m)
Weight 8 tons

Megaloceros giganteus (Giant deer)

Pronunciation
mega-low-sare-oss jie-gan-tee-us
Meaning Gigantic big-horn
Group Mammals—deer
Time Quaternary, 400,000 to 8,000 ya
Length 13 ft (4 m)
Weight 1,100 lb (500 kg)

Megalodon

Pronunciation
mega-low-don
Meaning Huge tooth
Group Sharks (selachians)
Time period Neogene, to 1.5 mya
Size 59 ft (18 m) long
Weight 55 tons

Meganeura

Pronunciation
mega-nure-ah
Meaning Big nerves or nets
Group Bugs
Time Carboniferous, 300 mya
Wingspan 29.5 in (75 cm)
Length 35.4 in (90 cm)

Megantereon

Pronunciation
meh-gan-ter-ee-on
Meaning Owen's big animal
Group Mammals—cats
Time Neogene and Quaternary, 4.5 million to 400,000 ya
Length 7.2 ft (2.2 m)
Weight 330 lb (150 kg)

Megateuthis

Pronunciation
mega-te-oo-this
Meaning Huge squid
Group Belemnites (molluscs)
Time period Jurassic, 150 mya
Size 10 ft (3 m) long
Weight About 176 lb (80 kg)

Megatherium (Giant ground sloth)

Pronunciation
mega-theer-ee-um
Meaning Great beast
Group Mammals—sloths and armadillos
Time Neogene and Quaternary, 5 million to 10,000 ya
Length 26 ft (8 m)
Weight 5.6 tons

Mosasaurus

Pronunciation
mow-za-saw-rus
Meaning Meuse lizard
Group Mosasaurs
Time period Late Cretaceous, 70 mya
Size 50 ft (15 m) long
Weight 22 tons

Ophiura

Pronunciation
off-ee-ure-a
Meaning Snake tail
Group Brittle stars and starfish (echinoderms)
Time period Ordovician, 480 mya
Size 20 in (50 cm) across
Weight 2.2 lb (2 kg)

Ornithocheirus

Pronunciation
or-nith-oh-kie-rus
Meaning Bird hand
Group Tailless pterosaurs
Time Late Cretaceous, 95 mya
Wingspan 20 ft (6 m)
Length 6.5 ft (2 m)

Orthoceras

Pronunciation
or-thow-seer-us
Meaning Straight horn
Group Nautiloids (mollusks)
Time period Silurian, 420 mya
Size 6.5 ft (2 m) long
Weight 110 lb (50 kg)

Palaeochiropteryx

Pronunciation
pale-ee-owe-kye-rop-tur-ix
Meaning Ancient hand wing
Group Bats
Time Mid Palaeogene, 47 mya
Wingspan 9.8 in (25 cm)
Length 3.9 in (10 cm)

Panderichthys

Pronunciation
pan-der-ich-this
Meaning Pander's fish
Group Fish—lobe-fins
Time Late Devonian, 380 mya
Length 3.9 ft (1.2 m)
Weight 33 lbs (15 kg)

Panthera Leo spelaea (Cave lion)

Pronunciation
pan-theera lee-oh spell-ee-a
Meaning Lion of the cave
Group Mammals—cats
Time Quaternary, 700,000 to 10,000 ya
Length 10 ft (3 m)
Weight 440 lbs (200 kg)

Paraceratherium

Pronunciation
para-seer-ah-theer-ee-um
Meaning Next to horn beast
Group Mammals—rhinos
Time Late Paleogene, Early Neogene, from 33 mya
Length 29.5 ft (9 m)
Weight 22 tons

Parapuzosia

Pronunciation
para-poo-zow-see-a
Meaning Alongside Puzos
Group Ammonites (mollusks)
Time period Late Cretaceous, 70 mya
Size 8.2 ft (2.5 m) across
Weight About 330 lb (150 kg)

Presbyornis

Pronunciation
prez-bee-orn-iss
Meaning Elder bird
Group Waterbirds
Time Early Palaeogene, 55 mya
Wingspan 6.5 ft (2 m)
Height 3.3 ft (1 m)

Protarchaeopteryx

Pronunciation
pro-tar-kee-op-tur-ix
Meaning Before Archaeopteryx
Group Dinosaurs
Time Early Cretaceous, 125 mya
Weight 8.8 lb (4 kg)
Length 3.3 ft (1 m)

Pteranodon

Pronunciation
tair-an-oh-don
Meaning Toothless wing
Group Tailless pterosaurs
Time Late Cretaceous, 70 mya
Wingspan Up to 29.5 ft (9 m)
Length 6.5 ft (2 m)

Pteraspis

Pronunciation
teh-rass-pis
Meaning Wing shield
Group Jawless fish (agnathans)
Time period Devonian, 400 mya
Size 7.9 in (20 cm) long
Weight About 17.7 oz (500 g)

Pterodaustro

Pronunciation
teh-row-dow-strow
Meaning South wind wing
Group Tailless pterosaurs
Time Mid-Cretaceous, 105 mya
Wingspan 8.2 ft (2.5 m)

Pterygotus

Pronunciation
teh-ree-go-tus
Meaning Winged animal
Group Sea scorpions (eurypterids)
Time period Silurian, 420 mya
Size 7.2 ft (2.2 m) long
Weight 154 lb (70 kg)

Quetzalcoatlus

Pronunciation
kwet-zal-coe-at-lus
Meaning After the Aztec god Quetzalcoatl
Group Tailless pterosaurs
Time Late Cretaceous, 70 mya
Wingspan 39 ft (12 m)
Length 20 ft (6 m)

Redlichia

Pronunciation
red-lick-ee-a
Meaning In honor of Hans Redlich
Group Trilobites
Time period Cambrian, 500 mya
Size Up to 20 in (50 cm) long
Weight 6.6 lb (3 kg)

Repenomamus

Pronunciation
rep-ee-no-mahm-us
Meaning Reptile mammal
Group Mammals— triconodonts
Time Early Cretaceous, 130 mya
Length 3.6 ft (1.1 m)
Weight 33 lb (15 kg)

Sarcosuchus

Pronunciation
sark-oh-sook-us
Meaning Flesh crocodile
Group Reptiles— crocodiles
Time Mid Cretaceous, 110 mya
Length 39 ft (12 m)
Weight 8.8 tons

Sarkastodon
Pronunciation
sar-kass-toe-don
Meaning Protector tooth
Group Mammals—creodonts
Time Paleogene, 36 mya
Length 9.8 ft (3 m)
Weight 1.1 tons

Scutosaurus
Pronunciation
scoo-toe-saw-rus
Meaning Shield reptile
Group Reptiles—anapsids
Time Late Permian, 252 mya
Length 8.2 ft (2.5 m)
Weight 1,100 lb (500 kg)

Shonisaurus
Pronunciation
shon-ee-saw-rus
Meaning Shoshone lizard
Group Ichthyosaurs
Time period Late Triassic, 210 mya
Size 65 ft (20 m) long
Weight 30 tons

Smilodon
Pronunciation
smile-oh-don
Meaning Chisel tooth
Group Mammals—cats
Time Quaternary, 1.8 million to 10,000 ya
Length 7.2 ft (2.2 m)
Weight 880 lb (400 kg)

Spriggina
Pronunciation
sprih-gee-nuh
Meaning In honor of Reg Sprigg
Group Probably worms (annelids)
Time period Ediacaran, 550 mya
Size 1.2 in (3 cm) long
Weight 1 oz (30g)

Teleoceras
Pronunciation
tell-ee-oh-seer-us
Meaning Distant horn
Group Mammals—rhinos
Time Neogene, 10 to 5 mya
Length 8.2 ft (2.5 m)
Weight 660 lb (300 kg)

Teratornis
Pronunciation
terra-tor-nis
Meaning Monster bird
Group Birds of prey
Time Quaternary, until 10,000 ya
Wingspan 11.8 ft (3.6 m)
Height 29.5 in (75 cm)

Thrinaxodon
Pronunciation
thrih-nax-uh-don
Meaning Three-pronged tooth
Group Mammal-like reptiles
Time Early Triassic, 245 mya
Length 15.8–20 in (40–50 cm)
Weight 6.6 lb (3 kg)

Thylacoleo
(Marsupial lion)
Pronunciation
thigh-la-coe-leo
Meaning Pouched lion
Group Mammals—marsupials
Time Quaternary, 2 million to 40,000 ya
Length 6.5 ft (2 m)
Weight 265 lb (120 kg)

Thylacosmilus
Pronunciation
thigh-la-cos-my-lus
Meaning Pouch sword
Group Mammals—marsupial-like
Time Neogene, 20 mya
Length 5 ft (1.5 m)
Weight 220 lb (100 kg)

Tiktaalik

Pronunciation
tick-taa-lick
Meaning Burbot fish
Group Fish—lobe-fins
Time Late Devonian, 375 mya
Length 8.2 ft (2.5 m)
Weight 165 lb (75 kg)

Titanis

Pronunciation
tie-tan-iss
Meaning Giant, titan
Group Birds—flightless
Time Late Neogene and
Early Quaternary, 5–2 mya
Height 8.3 ft (2.5 m)
Weight 375 lb (170 kg)

Titanophoneus

Pronunciation
tie-tan-oh-foe-nee-us
Meaning Giant killer
Group Mammal-like reptiles
Time Late Permian, 255 mya
Length 13 ft (4 m)
Weight 440 lb (200 kg)

Toxodon

Pronunciation
tock-sowe-don
Meaning Poison tooth
Group Mammals—hoofed
mammals
Time Quaternary, 2.6 million to
15,000 ya
Length 9 ft (2.7 m)
Weight 1 ton

Uintatherium

Pronunciation win-ta-theer-ee-um
Meaning Uinta beast
Group Mammals—dinoceratans
Time Paleogene, 40 mya
Length 14.8 ft (4.5 m)
Weight 2.2 ton

Ursus spelaeus (Cave bear)

Pronunciation
ur-suss spell-ee-us
Meaning Bear of the cave
Group Mammals—bears
Time Quaternary, 1 million to
27,000 ya
Length 10 ft (3 m)
Weight 1,100 lb (500 kg)

Xiphactinus

Pronunciation
ziff-act-eye-nus
Meaning Sword ray
Group Ray-finned fish
(actinopterygians)
Time period Late Cretaceous,
70 mya
Size 16.4 ft (5 m) long
Weight About 1,320 lb (600 kg)

GLOSSARY

Aetosaur A type of reptile that looked like a crocodile, but ate plants, with strong protective scales and horns.

Age of the Dinosaurs The time when dinosaurs were the main large land animals, from about 230 to 65 million years ago.

Amber Resin, a sticky liquid made by certain kinds of plants, which has gone hard over millions of years.

Ammonite A sea creature related to the octopus and squid, with big eyes, lots of tentacles, and a curly, snail-like shell. All ammonites have become extinct.

Amphibian An animal that lays its eggs in water, but lives most of its life on land.

Anthropornis A huge penguin, tall as an adult person, that lived 40 million years ago.

Antlers Large, hard, usually branched, hornlike parts growing from the top of a deer's head.

Anurognathus A small pterosaur, with wings about 16 inches (40 centimeters) across, which lived 150 million years ago.

Arachnid A member of the animal group that includes spiders, scorpions, mites, and ticks.

Belemnite A sea creature related to octopus and squid, with big eyes, lots of tentacles, and usually a cone-shaped shell. Belemnites are extinct now, but they have left many fossils.

Birds of prey Birds that hunt other creatures for food. Most have a sharp, hooked beak and long pointed claws called talons.

Breeding time When animals of the same kind get together to breed or produce young. For many creatures, this happens at a certain time of year, often spring.

Caudipteryx A small dinosaur, covered with birdlike feathers, that lived about 125 million years ago.

Cold-blooded A creature that cannot make body warmth inside itself, and so has a body temperature the same as its surroundings.

Creodonts Meat-eating animals similar to the cats, dogs, and hyenas of today, but which have all died out.

Crest Bone on the top of the head.

Dasornis A huge seabird with wings 16 feet (5 meters) across, probably a relative of today's geese and swans, that lived about 50 million years ago.

Dimorphodon An early kind of pterosaur from almost 200 million years ago, with wings 55 inches (140 centimeters) across and a long, trailing tail.

Drought A long period of dry weather, without rain or other forms of water.

Evolve To change gradually over a long period of time.

Extinct Not existing any more. An animal is extinct when all of its kind have died out.

Flightless birds Members of the bird group whose wings are too small to let them take off and fly.

Flying animals Creatures that can stay in the air for more than a couple of minutes and control their flight.

Fossil Any part of a plant or animal that has been preserved in rock. Also traces of plants or animals, such as footprints.

Hard-bodied animals Creatures with a hard outer body casing instead of an inside skeleton.

Hibernation When certain kinds of animals go into a long, deep sleep, usually to avoid difficult conditions such as the cold of winter.

Homo sapiens "Wise human," the scientific name for all the people alive today on Earth.

Icaronycteris One of the first bats, from almost 50 million years ago, with wings up to 16 inches (40 centimeters) across.

Ichthyornis A gull-like seabird from about 90–75 million years ago, with wings 20–24 inches (50–60 centimeters) across.

Ichthyosaur A sea-living, air-breathing reptile that looked similar to a dolphin, with paddle-shaped limbs and a swishy tail.

Jawless fish A fish that does not have jaw bones, but usually has a mouth like a sucker or slit.

Lobe-fin fish A fish with fins that have strong muscles in fleshy lumps or lobes at the base.

Mammal-like reptiles Animals that were partly like reptiles, and also partly like mammals, with fur or hair and warm blood. They have all died out.

Mammoth A large animal with a long nose trunk and two big tusks, similar to and closely related to the elephant and mastodon. All mammoths have become extinct.

Marsupial A mammal whose babies grow and develop in a pocket-like pouch on their mother's belly.

Mastodon A large animal with a long nose trunk and two tusks, similar to and closely related to the elephant and mammoth. All mastodons have become extinct. Mastodons were smaller than mammoths.

Meganeura A giant dragonfly-type bug with wings 30 inches (75 centimeters) across that lived 300 million years ago.

Mites Very small creatures with eight legs, which are close cousins of spiders.

Moas Huge birds that could not fly and once lived on the islands of New Zealand. They have all died out.

Mosasaur A sea-living, air-breathing reptile with paddle-like limbs and a large mouth with many big, sharp teeth.

Nautiloid A sea creature related to the octopus and squid, with big eyes, lots of tentacles, and a curly, snail-like shell.

Nose horns Horns that grow on the nose or snout, rather than on the top of the head.

Ornithocheirus A very big pterosaur that lived almost 100 million years ago in South America, with wings up to 20 feet (6 meters) across.

Plesiosaur A sea-living, air-breathing reptile with paddle-shaped limbs, a very long neck, and a small head.

Pliosaur A sea-living, air-breathing reptile with long paddle-shaped limbs, a big head, and huge mouth.

Predator An animal that hunts and kills other creatures, the prey, for its food.

Prehistoric time The time up to several thousand years ago, before people started to write down what happened as recorded history.

Presbyornis A tall, wading bird that walked along the seashore around 60–40 million years ago.

Prey A creature that is killed and eaten by another animal, the predator.

Primates A mammal group most of whose members have grasping hands and feet, big forward-facing eyes, and a long tail, and live in trees. Primates include lemurs, monkeys, apes, and humans.

Pteranodon One of the largest pterosaurs.

Pterosaurs Flying cousins of dinosaurs that lived at the same time, from about 225 to 65 million years ago. They had furry bodies and front limbs shaped like wings.

Ray-finned fish A fish with fins that have long, thin rods or rays holding them out.

Saber-toothed cats Cats with a pair of very long, curved, down-pointing teeth, shaped like the type of sword called a saber.

Sail-back A creature with a tall flap or extension of skin on its back.

Scavengers Animals that feed on dead bodies killed by other creatures, rather than killing them themselves.

Scutes Hard parts, like big scales, in an animal's skin that help to protect it.

Snowball Earth A time when much of planet Earth became very cold, with lots of snow and ice. Living things survived in only a few warmer parts of the world.

Spiny sharks Fish that looked like sharks, with sharp spines on their bodies for protection, but which were not in the main shark group.

Tar pits Places where thick, sticky tar or oil oozes naturally over the surface of the ground, forming a kind of black pool or lake where animals can become trapped and sink in.

Tetrapods Animals with four legs, or four limbs—two arms and two legs.

Top predator A big, hunting animal that can kill and eat most other creatures, and which no other animal would attack and eat.

Trilobite A sea-living creature with big eyes, a hard upper body shell, and many pairs of legs underneath.

True sharks Fish in the group that scientists call selachians, with a skeleton made not of bone but of cartilage or gristle.

Tusk A very big, long tooth that sticks out of the mouth.

INDEX